An Introduction

to

Information Technology

An Introduction to Information Technology

Anna Treby

CASSELL

Cassell
Wellington House
125 Strand, London WC2R 0BB

www.cassell.co.uk

370 Lexington Avenue
New York, NY 10017-6550

© Anna Treby 1998

All rights reserved. No part of this publication may be reproduced or transmitted in any form or by any means, electronic or mechanical including photocopying, recording or any information storage or retrieval system, without prior permission in writing from the publishers.

First published 1998

British Library Cataloguing-in-Publication Data
A catalogue record for this book is available from the British Library.

ISBN 0-304-70336-2

Designed and typeset by Barbara Linton in London W13.
Printed and bound in Great Britain by Redwood Books, Trowbridge, Wiltshire.

CONTENTS

Introduction		vii
Unit One		1
Unit Two		11
Unit Three		23
Unit Four		37
Unit Five		53
Unit Six		71
Unit Seven		93
Unit Eight		103
Appendices:		
(1)	Health and Safety – Display Ergonomics	120
(2)	Using Print Screen and Paintbrush	125
(3)	File Manager in Windows 3.1	129
(4)	Competence Statements	134
(5)	Personal and Witnessed Statements	138
(6)	Data Protection Act and EU Legislation	139
(7)	On Programme Tutorial Sheets	142
Glossary of NVQ and IT Terms and Abbreviations		146
NVQ Translation by Element		149
Supplementary Unit Scenarios		152
Bibliography, References and Acknowledgements		160

INTRODUCTION

Welcome to this book, which has been written especially with you, the student, in mind, and will, I hope, help you to achieve the award of NVQ Level II in Using Information Technology.

Firstly I want to answer some questions which you may have come up with yourself, and which arise very often from other students studying this syllabus.

What is an NVQ? (National Vocational Qualification)

An NVQ is a qualification based on standards, which have been developed by industry and commerce, and is awarded by bodies such as City and Guilds, RSA and the LCCI.

Each NVQ qualification is made up of a number of separate units, each one specifying exactly what must be achieved in order to attain it. Units can be thought of as 'milestones' or targets, which you achieve along the route to the overall award.

Each NVQ covers areas of competence specific to it. It is not exam based – it is a totally flexible way to study, with no time constraints, age limits or entry qualifications. In fact it is for everyone – including you, and will give you the edge over other people when in the job market!

Who is the NVQ Level II in Using IT for?

It is for those building towards competence in basic computer skills.

What is the NVQ Level II in Using IT made up of?

It is made up of 5 core units and 1 option module. The core units are numbered 1 to 5 and the options are 6, 7 and 8.

How is it assessed?

It is assessed through the demonstration of competence, over a period of time, which is associated with the criteria for each discreet unit.

How and where can I study for an NVQ qualification?

NVQs are work based qualifications, so you can study for them using your work placement and perhaps attending college for tuition on a day or evening release scheme.

or

Introduction

You could perhaps study for it on a full-time basis in colleges where the appropriate qualification is offered. You will need to find a part-time work placement to complement the course, so that you can apply your skills directly in the job that you do, and also gather information and evidence that you will need for your portfolio from both facilities.

What is evidence?

Evidence is the work that you do to show that you are competent and capable in a variety of different areas. It may be only a small part of your overall job, or a large part of your college course, it depends how and where you are studying for your award.

Evidence is often in the form of hardcopy – or paper printouts and documents, or it may be through signed witness or personal statements to authenticate the work that you have been producing.

Observation is also a major role, undertaken whilst you work on your NVQ award at college, and the lecturer will help you to gather evidence from the classes you attend.

What is a portfolio?

This is just another name for a file, which will hold all your work. Dividers usually split it up so that you can easily arrange all your work into their appropriate Units. (It is often easier to file your work as you go along, so that you can remember which Unit it belongs to, rather than have a massive pile to sort out at the end of your course.)

How will an NVQ help me in looking for a new job, or increase my prospects in my current one?

Employers like NVQs because they are work based/vocational qualifications which show a student's competence in a variety of skills, that are relevant to the type of work that they do. NVQs are practical proof that employees can do the tasks set and this is backed up by the appropriate qualifications given by the awarding bodies.

Training in any form helps to bring out the best in personnel. It will also increase their potential and enhance their contribution to the organisation as a whole, as well as ensure that they will do their job better. Personal, as well as organisational satisfaction, will be achieved and the overall workforce will work better together through the recognition that training and qualifications gives them. It will also improve their self-esteem and confidence, and measures and recognises their contribution to the organisation. Thousands of organisations are encouraging their personnel to undertake NVQ qualifications as they are recognised as being the most practical and beneficial way of achieving a competence and work based qualification, and one which also allows the work to continue whilst the workforce study.

Do I need to undertake work experience to achieve this qualification?

Most of the elements can be attained through a simulated working environment created for students who are studying the course at college. Elements 4.3 and 4.4 do, however, necessitate undertaking some real work in order to attain the required

Introduction

evidence. Work experience can cover a multitude of areas, and can be for anyone who requires some work to be done for them.

Sometimes colleges can place students in different departments around the facility, and get their students to perform a variety of IT related tasks which will ensure that they obtain the appropriate evidence that they need for these elements. Students studying the course on a part-time basis and who work the rest of the time have no difficulty in obtaining what they require from their normal working routine.

Liaison with both your lecturer and/or supervisor is essential early on in the course to establish how, when and where you will undertake a period of work experience, whether it will be on a 'one day a week' basis, or for a two week block later on in the course.

Personal contact with employers outside of the college is also a useful way to proceed, so that you, the student, can try to obtain work experience for yourself, rather than rely on the contacts and provision that the college may make for you. Employers are always glad to get an extra pair of hands, especially when they are free of charge. Often students who do the work experience in an outside organisation are offered permanent positions once the course is over, so it is a good opportunity to get a foot in the door.

Some students prefer to do one day a week because of family commitments, but be warned – often the employer leaves all the same tasks for you to do, on the same day that you go in each week. This can result in a rather limited experience and also a lack of evidence for your portfolio. It is often better to attend for a whole two weeks and get a better and more rounded picture of what the job entails. It will also mean that you will be able to finish something that you started the day before, rather than have to shelve it for the next week, or pass it on to someone else for completion.

Work out your weekly commitments, liaise with your lecturer/supervisor early on in the course, use old contacts and write to employers who you feel would be interested in your help, and also people who *you* would like to work for after you have qualified. Be prepared to do anything relevant, and to obtain as much evidence as you can for inclusion in your portfolio. It is also an ideal opportunity to try out a variety of jobs new to you, and to see if you would like to do them on a permanent basis.

Having now answered some of the questions you may have been asking yourself, I can fill you in on the format that this book will take.

(1) The Performance Criteria, Range Statement and Evidence Required for each element within each unit are outlined, according to the standards body – ITITO – and will be detailed at the beginning of each element.

(2) Each unit is then tackled and explained in a practical way that is easy to understand, illustrating some of the aspects which have to be covered in order to achieve it.

(3) Each unit has an exercise, which, if undertaken, will pull all the loose threads of the unit together. You should not use this exercise in isolation, but as an addition to the other evidence you produce in order to fulfil the requirements of the standards.

(4) Illustrations and examples may be detailed to explain the requirements of the unit.

Introduction

(5) Further scenario exercises are offered in the Appendices for those eager to tackle more complex situations, and these may be familiar from the office/IT scene within today's working world.

At the back of the book and covered in the Appendices section, are a number of topics which have been covered in depth so as to add extra information. These can be utilised and included in the appropriate units throughout the syllabus. (See the Table of Contents for further details on subjects covered in this way.)

I hope that you will find this book to be of help to you as you travel on your educational journey, seeking information and producing evidence for the overall award. I have piloted much of the work and exercises with my current students who are undertaking this course, and trust that you will continue, like them, to strive and seek a satisfactory end result.

GOOD LUCK!

ANNA TREBY

BA.(Hons), AMBCS., AIMgt, MInstAM(AdvDip), MIQPS., MABAC

Lecturer in Administration, Business, Computing and Management

UNIT 1

ELEMENT 1

Prepare use of information technology

Performance criteria

(a) Use of IT solution to meet customer requirements is accurately established.

(b) Equipment and materials are selected to meet customer requirements.

(c) Equipment is set up correctly in line with regulations.

(d) Software is selected and accessed in accordance with regulations.

(e) Sources of data are correctly identified and, when outside own authority, verified.

Range statement

(1) MATERIALS Magnetic media, consumables.

(2) EQUIPMENT Installed supplied processor, installed supplied input device, installed supplied output device.

(3) SOFTWARE Pre-installed application software, system software.

(4) REGULATIONS Organisation's legislation, health and safety, equipment manufacturer's, software supplier's.

Evidence required

Details of customer requirements.

Observation of the candidate at work over a period of time preparing the hardware for use and selecting the required materials.

Evidence for this element may come from a realistic working environment.

Questioning is used where necessary to confirm specified knowledge.

The information detailed here covers all the elements necessary for you to successfully complete and attain Unit 1. Some questions or exercises are indicated as we go along and are typed in *italics*.

Try to make notes about each subject covered as you come across it within your college or work placement tasks, so that at the end of the unit completion of the Competence Statement will not be so time-consuming or difficult. It is often a good idea to have extra copies of the blank forms to hand so that you can jot down the elements you cover as you go, and then just rewrite/type your notes for a comprehensive and well documented statement.

For attainment of this element, you need to be able to use floppy disks, and know how to format them if you use the unformatted variety, although these seem to be a rarity these days. It also means being able to put correct information onto a disk label so that it is easy to find the files you may need in the future.

You need to know the process, as applicable to your establishment, for logging in to your computer, and the procedures and regulations that are necessary to utilise, so that correct and appropriate security is ensured at all times. Similarly, it is necessary to be able to shut down the computer when you have finished using it, so that it is either ready for another user, if you have shared facilities, or for you to resume work at another time. This is especially important when you are using the Windows operating system, or specific passwords, which unless you log-out correctly may hinder your access at another time.

Note what you have to do to log in and out of your computer. Why is this necessary?

Most equipment that you utilise will already be set up and correctly configured for your use, either at work or college, so there is no real need to know about **all** the intricacies of how to put it together. On the other hand, as more and more of us are now purchasing computers for use at home, we do need to know something about which bit fits where, and how to install additional software!

Most of the computers available 'off the shelf' today are what are termed as 'plug in and play': that means that all you have to do is literally plug it in and off you go. This does seem rather too simple, and often terminology and complex information stumps us should we wish to develop our system further by adding to the hardware or software. Making additions tends to require more time and ability to understand the directions and the manuals which accompany the new products. Some basic ability therefore needs to be taught, and the simplest instructions given to everyone so that we are all competent with the setting up of a computer. Normally this is undertaken as part of a course whilst in college, but often it is a case of being thrown in at the deep end in a working situation. It is often better to seek assistance from those better qualified, or with greater knowledge than yourself, rather than to tackle something which may not have the desired outcome, and may cause even greater problems in the long run.

Another aspect which has to be addressed at this junction, concerns Health and Safety. (This aspect ripples through the whole of this syllabus, and will be covered in depth later on.) This is not just for your own personal protection, again either within the establishment where you are a student, or within the workplace as an employee, but to safeguard others who study/work alongside you, but also to ensure that the law and its requirements are upheld.

What requirements do you know about and why are they necessary?

Unit 1

Where computers are concerned, there is much to facilitate, and this is tackled in more detail within the Appendices section at the back of the book. You need to be Health and Safety conscious for yourself and for others, so always TAKE CARE!

Access to the software within the computer system is usually set up by the computer department, or the administrator, thus ensuring that everyone has the appropriate rights and privileges that they need to perform their job correctly. This also helps to safeguard the data stored on the system and will maintain its overall security. Rules and regulations are often distributed to new students/personnel so that they are aware of the restrictions that apply, and what the consequences are should they disobey them. Often this means that you cannot play games on the computers, or access the Internet without prior authorisation. Penalties and punishments may not only affect those who disregard the rules, but everyone within the establishment as well!

What are some of the requirements within your college/workplace?

Finally, it is always important to remember that when you work on a computer you use the correct application to do the job, that you establish the exact requirements from the 'customer' who gives you the task, and that you perform all the operations required within the confines of both the establishment and/or manufacturer's guidelines.

Saved files need to be correctly named using the appropriate conventions applicable to both the system that you use and also the house style that is utilised. The creation of directories and the performance of good 'housekeeping' are all necessary to ensure the long-term safety and security of the system and the work that you generate.

Knowledge of the system and how it is set up is also a good thing, so that you can utilise the appropriate facilities and store your work in the correct directory or drive. It may be that others need to access the information that you enter, and that their access is only possible if you store it in a specific place. Identification of these files may also need to be done in a predetermined fashion, so that it is easy to identify the latest file through the incorporation of the date into the name, or the type of file, through the file extension, e.g. *.let* for a letter. There are numerous ways and means of identification, and you will need to ascertain the appropriate method used and note where and how you save your files.

Always remember that the rules, regulations and restrictions exist for your benefit and if in doubt, seek authorisation or clarification before you proceed.

Where would you go for guidance and advice about computer regulations and restrictions?

ELEMENT 2

Monitor use of information technology

Performance criteria

(a) Working environment is monitored against regulations.

(b) Health and safety requirements are followed at all times.

(c) Appropriate records selected for updating are completed correctly and legibly.

(d) System integrity and security is preserved at all times.

(e) Materials selected are correctly used.

(f) Errors are correctly identified and dealt with in accordance with regulations.

Range statement

(1) WORKING ENVIRONMENT   Equipment, software, furniture, cabling.

(2) SPECIFIED REQUIREMENTS Own authority, outside own authority.

(3) REGULATIONS Organisation's, legislation, equipment manufacturer's, software supplier's, health and safety.

(4) RECORDS   Work sheets, error logs, maintenance records.

(5) SYSTEM   Hardware, software, data.

(6) MATERIALS   Data, magnetic media, consumables.

(7) ERRORS   Within own authority, outside own authority.

Evidence required

Two types of records as stated in range.

Observation of the candidate at work over a period of time performing to regulations.

Evidence for this element may come from a realistic working environment.

Questioning is used where necessary to confirm specified knowledge.

This element deals mainly with the continuing use of the computer and its facilities within the day-to-day environment in which you use it. It incorporates the usage of passwords to protect the work that you do as well as the overall facilities that the system offers to everyone. It will ensure that passwords and security facilities are maintained continuously and that changes are implemented as appropriate.

Every system will develop problems and faults and it is necessary for everyone to be aware of the correct procedures to follow should one occur. It may be that you need to call the technicians in for an immediate repair, or, if only a minor setback, to complete

Unit 1

the appropriate forms or make a phone call to the computer department, where the fault is logged and a reference number given, so that all errors and faults can be monitored and corrected in turn. Whatever the system that your facility utilises, it is necessary to follow the procedures and this will also help to maintain a safe working environment.

What facilities are in place for fault or error reporting that you know about?

As mentioned earlier, Health and Safety appears all over the place, and here we need to keep a constant check on cables, screens and other working parts of the computers we use so that we can be certain that they are in perfect working order at all times, and that no harm can come to the users as a result of negligence. Keeping the equipment clean and free from dust is an important aspect of the user's routine and it will also help to prolong the life of the machine itself. Appropriate Health and Safety measures need to be implemented here so as to maintain your own personal safety.

What should you check regularly to ensure that you have a hazard free computer to work on?

Often when computers are serviced or repaired, like a car with its routine services, a log is kept, so that it is possible to isolate machines which have recurring problems, or that need extra maintenance as a matter of course. The utilisation of a database facility is often a good way to monitor faults and maintenance for each machine. Similarly, this can be used to log all the software that you have, and what is installed on each machine or server on a network. It may also record the types of licence that each application has, date originally purchased and from whom, dates of any upgrades and current versions available and on which machines; all of this is useful data when maintaining an efficient and organised computer facility.

How is the software logged where you study/work?

Worksheets can also be produced to detail the work that you, the user, undertake each day, so that you can see at a glance exactly what has been done, where to find it and who it was produced for. Often this recording facility will help to ascertain where the bulk of your work comes from, and may even perhaps offer the opportunity for additional time or facilities to ensure that all the work is done according to the 'customer' requirements. Progress can also be recorded in this fashion, and it may be beneficial for the student to keep a diary, or a log of what you are set and the dates that it has to be in by, so that you do not miss any crucial deadlines. It will also help to monitor your progress through the course, and to establish where you are at any time. The 'targets' or 'milestones' mentioned in the introduction can be recorded on a chart, or a timetable/scheme of work, which will show you what you have achieved and what you have left to do.

Perhaps this is a good opportunity to produce such a chart or plan, so that you can monitor your progress from here, and set yourself some deadlines to work to, so that you will be able to finish the course in good time. Think of the best way to show how this could be done, and produce some ideas using the most appropriate software to give a meaningful end result. Keep a blank copy of what you originally produce for your portfolio, and also completed ones that you do at different stages through your course, so that you have graphical evidence of your continual progress.

Throughout your use of the computer, it is necessary to implement certain appropriate 'housekeeping' procedures and routines so that if there is a serious problem with the system, you will be able to recreate your work with very little effort. Always keep a back up of your files on a floppy disk, if you work to the hard drive or network, or vice versa. All floppy disks and original software disks and CD ROMs need to be kept in a fireproof safe, or off site, so that if there is a fire, or other major emergency, then all the work generated is safe and can be reutilised when the system is functioning again.

What 'housekeeping' procedures do you implement – daily, weekly, monthly?

Always make sure that you know where to go for help, which manuals or booklets to read, and where they are located. Follow any rules and regulations so that you will have a problem free time using the computer.

ELEMENT 3

Conclude use of information technology

Performance criteria

(a) All necessary working data are saved conforming to organisation's standards and are in the correct location.

(b) Files are secured correctly and completely to a remote physical location.

(c) Redundant files within own authority are deleted.

(d) Redundant files outside of own responsibility are dealt with in accordance with instructions.

(e) Materials to be unloaded are identified and stored in designated location.

(f) Only those aspects of the system within authority are closed down.

Range statement

(1) DATA Files, sources.

(2) SECURITY REQUIREMENTS Organisation's, legislation, manufacturer's software.

(3) MATERIALS Magnetic media, consumables.

(4) SYSTEM Hardware, software.

Evidence required

Printouts detailing file locations before and after deletions.

Observation of the candidate at work over a period of time.

Evidence for this element may come from a realistic working environment.

Questioning is used when necessary to confirm specified knowledge.

Unit 1

This final element in Unit 1 helps the user to maintain a state of readiness for the next time that they use the computer. It entails the closing down of open facilities and applications and leaving the computer in a state of safety with all the data secure within.

We have discussed the use of 'housekeeping' routines and procedures to make the most effective use of the storage space within the computer, if it is a stand alone PC, and also to have some method of monitoring the time that you keep files for. For some establishments it may be a requirement of law that you have both traceability and access for five or seven years. This may mean many files being stored on your system, and it may be necessary to provide a facility whereby they are stored on a magnetic medium, or other consumable material so as not to take up space on your working facility and which may well slow down its processing power and other capabilities, as well as hinder the storage of any current work.

Where and how do you store your 'old' files, and for how long?

Deletion of old files may need to be monitored so that you can see exactly which ones need to go and when.

'Housekeeping' is an essential part of the use of a computer and needs to be carefully monitored. A good way of recording the processes that you use, especially for the evidence you need for this course, is to use Print Screen when in File Manager or Explorer, paste it into PAINT, cut out the bits you do not need and then import it into Word. This will accurately reflect all the directories and files that you have access to and will then after deletion, through using the process again, show what is left. This is a very useful facility, and one which is documented in greater detail in the Appendices section at the back of this book.

Detail your personal directories before and after sorting them out.

Always remember to close down the computer when you have finished using it, with the correct procedures, and not by just turning it off. Save your work regularly, and use the appropriate naming conventions so that you can find it again in the future.

Throughout this syllabus it is useful to seek the authentication of any work undertaken that you may wish to include in your portfolio, and to do this either seek the help of your lecturer or your supervisor. Observation plays an important part in the early days of this course, and the lecturer will monitor carefully your progress throughout. Work undertaken in the work place, and not observed by the lecturer, will have to be authenticated by your supervisor, and this can be successfully achieved by the production of Witness Statements, or Personal Statements, which document the task undertaken and are signed off by those in authority who can safely say that it was all your own work.

Witness Statements are those written and signed by someone who witnessed the whole process that you undertook. A Personal Statement is one which you have written and someone else signs to say that what you have declared is correct. Both forms are useful when compiling evidence to substantiate the work undertaken to achieve this award.

Produce suitable Statements to authenticate your work.

CONCLUSION

Enable use of information technology solution

Completion of this Unit will demonstrate that you can:

- Use appropriate hardware and software to undertake any given task;
- Monitor work and maintain your computer;
- Sort out any minor errors or faults, and if this is not possible, adopt the appropriate procedures to do so;
- Save and name files according to the conventions applicable to you;
- Close down the computer correctly, and leave it ready for the next user, or your resumption at a later date.

CONGRATULATIONS – YOU HAVE NOW SUCCESSFULLY COMPLETED UNIT ONE!

To tie up all the loose ends covered in this Unit, try to complete the Unit 1 exercise to produce additional evidence for inclusion in your portfolio.

EXERCISE

Provide a comprehensive document to cover the following aspects which make up the basis of Unit 1 – Prepare Use of Information Technology; Monitor Use of Information Technology; Conclude Use of Information Technology.

(1) In your college or workplace, make a list of all the different types of computer in use and whether they use Windows 3.1 or Windows '95 operating systems. List all the software loaded or available on each different type of computer. Certain rooms/departments may use specialist software. If so, detail this and what it is used for. Also, look at the storage facilities linked to each computer. Do you save your work to a floppy disk, the hard drive, or a special place allocated to you on the network, for use whilst working/studying? (Don't duplicate information if every machine has the same software on it, just state it once and give the reasons why.)

N.B. The easiest way to document this information is to construct a table and insert all the information for each computer across several columns. See the example below.

Unit 1

Computer type	Location	Operating system	Storage medium	Software loaded/available	Comments
OPUS 486	ROOM 320	WINDOWS 3.1	Floppy disk or G: drive on the network.	MICROSOFT OFFICE PROFESSIONAL	Computer classroom

or

Computer type	Location	Operating system	Storage medium	Software loaded/available	Comments
OPUS 486	SALES DEPT	WINDOWS '95	Floppy disk or hard drive for personal work, general information saved to the networked drive facility.	MICROSOFT OFFICE PROFESSIONAL	General usage by all staff dealing with sales enquiries and invoices

(2) Investigate the procedures in place for users to 'log in' and 'log out' of the computers. Give details of any password facilities – max./min. number of characters to use, and how often you have to change them. Detail any security measures in place to maintain the integrity of the system and associated software in use.

(3) Document what 'housekeeping' or back-up procedures or routines are instigated or advised, both on a personal and organisational level, and their frequency.

(4) Health and Safety needs to be considered at all levels. What measures can you see that are taken to ensure your personal health and safety, as well as that of your colleagues? Document any areas which you feel are substandard, or that need to be implemented. What measures are in place for the security and safety of the software? (Cover copyright, manufacturers' legislation, software licences and organisational restrictions and procedures which may be in place.) Investigate manual and automatic virus checking routines and explain the necessity of them.

(5) Detail what you would do if your machine developed an error or fault. Also detail what you would do if you had a hardware problem and why. Some hardware problems may include failure to boot up, screen failure, non-functioning mouse, or a locked keyboard.

UNIT 2

ELEMENT 1

Enter data to create and update files

Performance criteria

(a) Authority to access files and data is obtained as necessary.

(b) Files required to be updated are correctly identified and located.

(c) Existing data to be updated is correctly identified, located and conforms to requirements.

(d) Data is entered using appropriate device completely, correctly and to schedule.

(e) Appropriate use is made of data checking facilities.

(f) Files created or updated are saved conforming to agreed or organisation's standards.

Range statement

(1) FILE New, existing.

(2) REQUIREMENTS Specified, unspecified.

(3) DATA Number, text.

(4) DEVICE Keyboard, selection device.

(5) ORGANISATION'S STANDARDS Naming convention, locating, frequency.

Evidence required

Printouts detailing file locations and showing updated data.

Observation of the candidate at work over a period of time entering data.

Evidence for this element may come from a realistic working environment.

Questioning is used where necessary to confirm specified knowledge.

The information detailed here covers all the elements necessary for you to successfully complete and attain Unit 2. Some questions or exercises are indicated as we go along and are typed in *italics*.

Enter data to create and update files

Try to make notes about each subject covered as you come across it within your college or work placement tasks, so that at the end of the Unit completion of the Competence Statement will not be so time-consuming or difficult. It is often a good idea to have extra copies of the blank forms to hand so that you can jot down the elements you cover as you go, and then just rewrite/type your notes for a comprehensive and well documented statement.

This element is all about locating and identifying files, using the File Manager or explorer, entering data to update or create new files, and the general construction and saving of the files that you create as part of your daily routine, either whilst you are at college, or within your work placement.

Whatever software and operating system you use, the facilities and requirements are fundamentally the same. It is essential to understand what needs to be created or updated, where it is located and where to save the edited file to, so that it is available for other users, or yourself in the future.

> *Where do you find the files that you need to update? Write out the path to get there and how you achieve this.*

If you are editing an existing document, you need to ascertain its filename and location, so that you can access it. If you are set this task within the realms of your work placement, and can utilise the hardcopy proof for evidence in your portfolio – check that it is not confidential or contains sensitive material first – print it out in its original form first so that you can see just what the editing you do consists of, and how it has progressed from start to finish.

Every document that you produce needs to be carefully proofread and checked to make sure that it is exactly what was required and that there are no spelling or grammatical errors. (Some software today offers you the facility of checking your spelling and grammar on screen, by underlining the incorrect words and/or phrases. This helps you to produce well written and spelt documents, but always spend a couple of minutes at the end double checking that you have not omitted any words, or incorrectly written the information, thus giving it the wrong interpretation or emphasis.)

> *Which button on the toolbar helps you to check if you have put any extra spaces or carriage returns into your word-processed document so that it does not use the word-wrap facility properly?*

Saving files may mean using a floppy disk, hard drive or network facility, whatever has been set up for this purpose. Naming conventions may be used to formulate easily interpreted names for files, or may include dates, initials or numbers to keep track of the number of documents that are produced. Some organisations have their own format for saving files and you need to conform to these.

> *What convention do you conform to?*

If no house style is specified, then develop one of your own. Start by creating directories on your floppy disk so that you can easily find the files that you create. It may be as simple as calling them letters, memos and reports and putting the same type of document into the correct directory.

> *What directories could you set up, and what would you call them?*

Unit 2

If you are using Windows 3.1, then the file naming convention offers you the facility of up to 8 characters before the file extension at the end. Remember not to include spaces or punctuation in your file name, as the computer will not be able to comprehend what you are trying to do, use letters and numbers only. Most software automatically puts on the appropriate extension that it generates – e.g. *.doc* – WORD, *xls* – EXCEL. You can however alter these extensions to fit your own needs, and you may want to include ones such as *.let* – LETTER, *.bak* – backup. Whatever you decide to use, stick to it so that you do not become confused and you conform to your own convention and standard, or those of the college or workplace that you are generating the work for.

The simple way of keeping all your files in order and up-to-date is, as previously detailed, through the use of appropriate directories for the work that you generate. More detail is given in the Appendices at the back of the book.

Once you have created your directories and know what naming conventions you need to use, it is all plain sailing from then, but you do need to remember to keep your files tidy, and to delete, move or copy old ones to other directories so that others can access them if required, or just to keep the directories current and not full of obsolete and no longer required files. It may be useful to create a directory called 'archive', so that you can place all your files that are out of date, but which you may need to retain for future use. Many organisations have a method of storing old files on magnetic tape, or in special archive areas where they can be stored for all time, but in such a way that they will not impede the processing power of the computer or its required capabilities.

Make regular saves of your work, just in case there is a problem with your computer/system, as it is surprising how much work you can generate in a few minutes, and this can easily be lost in the case of a crash or power surge. Make backup copies of your floppy disks, especially if you are doing detailed or complex work, so that you have a copy to fall back on in an emergency. You can also make back-ups of the files you save to the hard disk or network facility. It is always better to be safe than sorry!

> *Find out about the automatic saving facility on your computer and set it to save every five minutes. Document the process you utilised.*

If you are using an existing document and are not sure if what you are doing is correct, save the file with a different filename, thus leaving the original intact, and then if necessary you always have the original left to redo the work on. If, however, what you are doing is correct, then you can use it and rename it so that it follows the original format. This will just overwrite the original file and no one will be the wiser, you can always delete the extra file from the directory when you have had confirmation that your work is correct.

If you use other people's work for updating, make sure that you use the correct files and that you have their authority to do so.

Many of these facilities fall into the facility termed as 'housekeeping'. They are all simple but effective measures to ensure that all your work is safe and up-to-date, and that you operate an efficient and accurate computer system.

ELEMENT 2

Produce required document by manipulating

Performance criteria

(a) Customer document requirements are accurately established, verified and checked.

(b) Options for document layout and data formatting are identified and preferred solution agreed with customer.

(c) Document handling facilities to input, select and combine stored data are correctly used to meet requirements.

(d) Facilities are used correctly and efficiently to structure the required document.

(e) Facilities are used correctly and efficiently to layout and format the required document.

(f) Document is checked to be complete and error free.

Range statement

(1) DATA Text, graphic image, numeric.

(2) LAYOUT Page size, page orientation, page numbering, headers, footers, columns.

(3) FORMAT Text: Appearance, margins, indent, tabs, paragraphs. Graphic: Size, orientation, position.

(4) DOCUMENT HANDLING FACILITIES Merge, sort, retrieve.

(5) STRUCTURE FACILITIES Indexing, paragraph numbering, table of contents.

Evidence required

Three documents produced, each combining at least two data types, covering the range.

Details of customer requirement.

Observation of the candidate at work over a period of time producing documents.

Evidence for this element may come from a realistic working environment.

Questioning is used where necessary to confirm specified knowledge.

Manipulating data means utilising the capabilities and facilities available today in a variety of software packages to formulate the most appropriate document to meet the needs of the customer.

Such facilities include mail merge, sorting of tables or data, 'find and replace' or any facility using the integration of packages or the handling of the data within a document, as described through utilising the processes above.

Sorting of tables and data can be dealt with on a small scale initially to get the process correct, and such automated facilities will help us to appreciate the way in which technology assists us in our everyday working life.

Text, numbers and graphics can all be dealt with successfully in many word-processing packages if alternative specialist software is not available. Databases also happily manipulate data, sort and search for the answers to the questions or queries posed.

The appearance of a document often needs to be considered prior to you starting to key in the information. You may need to answer some basic questions first. Which way round should I use the paper? Portrait or landscape? What size font should I use? How big should my margins be?

> *Consider all the questions posed above and apply to the following document: A large table detailing all the staff in an organisation (100 employees) and their names, addresses and telephone numbers.*

Some forethought may help to alleviate much aggravation later on and will also help to save time.

Let us consider some of the terminology used here.

What is meant by the words PORTRAIT and LANDSCAPE?

Portrait is the most widely used page orientation for letters, memos, reports and documents in general. Consider however, a large table, a spreadsheet or graphic and how much better this will fit onto a page turned the other way around – landscape. These two options are available in most software packages, and it is necessary for you to ascertain how to change your page layout, and when to use them both appropriately. It is possible to create a document in its entirety using just one layout, as well as to change just the orientation of a specific page somewhere in the body of the document in order to facilitate a table or spreadsheet. Most spreadsheet and database information looks better printed out in landscape format, but if there is a choice you should be aware of how to select the option you require.

> *Change the orientation of your document from portrait to landscape for the whole of its length. Plus, change just one page in the middle of a word-processed document to accommodate a table or large graphic. Write down where you found the facility to change the orientation as well as how you achieved it.*

Margins, tabs and indents in a word-processed document help the layout to look professional, conform to house styles and make them generally easier to read. It may be that you need to break up the contents of the document into manageable chunks, or to highlight specific topics or facilitate headings within its structure.

Set up a series of tabs within the body of a document to enable you to key in the arrival and departure times for a travel itinerary you have been asked to compile for some members of your department/college course. Make up the venues as befitting and arrange it neatly onto the page orientation of your choice.

The style of reports and forms in databases is set for you to construct. Again, more forethought is required so that the end result conforms and meets your personal needs or organisational requirements.

Special facilities for paragraph numbering, indexing and the automatic creation of a Table of Contents in a word-processing package should also be looked into, so that you are aware of facilities which minimise additional work where possible and get the computer to use its sophisticated facilities and do the hard work for you!

Other facilities, which may be useful in the course of working with documents, are headers and footers. Some organisations have their address and phone number detailed in a header facility, which can be accessed for every document generated. It may be that you have a house style to use to produce departmental documents, or just that you need to put your name and examination number on every piece of paper that you produce in an exam, so that the printouts are taken to the correct student. Through the utilisation of the header and footer facility you need only type in the information once per document. (Note: when you create a header or footer, it will not be seen on your normal view of the document on the screen, it is only visible when you go into Page Preview.)

Identify where you will find the header and footer facility on your word-processing package, and produce a document to illustrate its use successfully.

Many of us belong to clubs and societies that produce newsletters or information sheets, and these are often created using the facilities available within software today. They look very professional when produced in column format and can include graphics or charts to illustrate the text.

Produce a newsletter in two columns to illustrate this facility. Include suitable graphics and detail how you achieved the end result.

Integration of documents, or the utilisation of sections of documents produced in other applications, may help to prevent duplication of work, and may also offer the opportunity to develop a more professional look to the overall document, especially when a graphical representation demonstrates a point that you are making.

Produce a document to show clearly the possible integration of one document type with another. Detail what you had to do to obtain the end result.

The scope available today is tremendous, and all it takes is a little forethought and preparation, plus the ability to use the applications to their fullest potential.

Unit 2

ELEMENT 3

Output specified document to destination

Performance criteria

(a) Appropriate destination is correctly selected.

(b) The destination device is checked to ensure that it is able to receive output.

(c) Document is checked to be complete and correct prior to output.

(d) Output parameters are identified and set up correctly to meet output requirements.

(e) Document is output to correct destination.

(f) Output is checked to be complete and meets the customer's requirements.

Range statement

(1) DESTINATION DEVICE Hardcopy, magnetic storage.

(2) OUTPUT PARAMETERS Page range, number of copies, print definition.

Evidence required

Three documents output covering both destination devices.

Details of customer requirement.

Observation of the candidate at work over a period of time producing output.

Evidence for this element may come from a realistic working environment.

Questioning is used where necessary to confirm specified knowledge.

Once you have completed your document and checked it thoroughly for spelling and grammatical errors, as well as making sure that it meets all the specified requirements and criteria given to you, you can think about printing it out.

Firstly check and make sure that your computer is linked to a printer, either directly, through a T-switch facility, or through a network connection. Ensure that there is sufficient paper to print your entire document, and that the toner or ink facility is adequate to meet your needs. Some documents require both a black and colour cartridge to print out any coloured text, charts or graphics you may have included in your document, so check both – run a short test sheet to do this.

Output specified document to destination

Produce a suitable test sheet to check the ink in your printer, for both black and colour, if is it available.

If your computer is linked into a switch box, or a T-switch facility, make sure that the knob is turned to the appropriate letter or number for your computer, so that the data you transmit when you press the print button, or select File -> Print, will be received in full and can print out the information that it receives.

How is your computer connected to the printer?

Some printers utilise several trays of paper. This can be clearly seen when printing long letters. The first sheet is normally for headed paper and will come from one tray of the printer. Any continuation pages will be just plain paper, or with an address across the bottom, and will come from a different tray. It is necessary to make sure that you set up your output requirements to meet these needs.

Always check to make sure that the printer is switched on and that it is 'on-line'. This means that it is ready for use, and if it is not, will not print out the document as required.

More than one copy can be printed by increasing the number of copies required within the Print facility. Each document is printed in full, and when complete it moves on to the next copy and so on, until it has finished printing the required amount.

Often we detect an error, or an additional amendment is required in a document that we have produced. Sometimes we can get away with just printing out again the affected pages, rather than reprinting the whole of the document from scratch. To be able to do this you can use a couple of different methods.

Firstly, you can go into FILE -> Print and select Current Page. This will print out just the page where your cursor is. Make sure that this really is the right page. If not, move your cursor to the correct page and then use the Current Page option again.

Secondly you can print out a selection of several different pages, and again not the whole document. Go into FILE -> Print, and this time select the Pages option. In the box to the right, type in the page numbers that you require to be reprinted. Separate individual page numbers with a comma, or specify ranges by typing in the start and finish numbers separated by a dash/hyphen. If more than one set of these pages is required, increase the Copies Required facility appropriately.

If you use the printer button on the toolbar, you will generate a complete copy of the whole document, rather than just what you require, so remember to use the appropriate facility to accommodate your requirements, and be environmentally friendly in the process!

Which option do you use most and why?

Save your document when you have completely finished your editing, using the appropriate naming convention that you are familiar with. When you come to close your file, if you have not saved it recently, or the last set of amendments you made, it will prompt you to save it before it closes it. This is a gentle reminder from the computer to make sure that you do not lose any work, and that it all remains safe and secure for future use.

Unit 2

CONCLUSION

Produce documents using information technology solution

This Unit looks closely at the whole cycle of creating a document, from its humble beginnings to its final printed form, using a variety of concepts and facilities to give it a really professional finish.

Whatever the type of document you are creating, whether for yourself or someone else, consider the task thoroughly, make sure that you use the most appropriate software for the task and that you have all you need to hand so that you can complete the task successfully. Finalise all the details with the 'customer' beforehand, and discuss any relevant details as necessary. Approach the task with enthusiasm and confidence. Use the best application available, and keep checking that what you are doing fits the bill. Produce draft copies for checking and get the final version approved before it is handed in/submitted or distributed to others. When it has been sent off, it is too late to retrieve it and sort out any errors that you may find at the last minute.

Spend some time checking for errors of spelling and grammar; consider also the way it looks. It is much more satisfying to produce a well presented and professional document than something that was hurriedly thrown together.

Completion of this Unit will demonstrate that you can:

- Enter data in a variety of software packages;
- Check the data for errors;
- Save and name files appropriately;
- Use page orientation and size to change the look of your document;
- Add columns, headers and footers as appropriate;
- Change the format of your document using margins, tabs and indents;
- Retrieve files and sort data;
- Add tables of contents and paragraph numbers;
- Print your document.

> CONGRATULATIONS – YOU HAVE NOW SUCCESSFULLY COMPLETED UNIT TWO!

To tie up all the loose ends covered in this Unit, try and complete the Unit 2 exercise to produce additional evidence for inclusion in your portfolio.

EXERCISE

The document generated by this exercise covers the elements which make up Unit 2 – Enter data to create and update files; Produce required document by manipulating data; Output specified document to destination.

You work for an organisation which makes computer games. They're just about to launch a new game in time for the Christmas market.

You have been asked to design an **A4, 3 column flyer in landscape format** to promote the new game. One side of the flyer is to promote the new game and should include some relevant and interesting graphics; the other side is to give details about the organisation (make these up) and should contain a graph or piechart to show the organisation's growth over the past few years.

Indent the first line of each paragraph of text by 1.5cm; include a header which contains the organisation's name in CAPITAL LETTERS, and a footer which details the name of the new game and the words 'AVAILABLE SOON'. Spell and grammar check the contents before printing out the final version of the flyer.

Design your document manually at first to save time and errors later and include your draft versions in your portfolio to show your document's progress from start to finish. Save the document on to a floppy disk as you go. Regular saves will ensure that you do not lose any important or intricate work. Call the file **'flyer'** so that you can refer to it for future use.

This exercise can be as simple or as detailed as you wish - ENJOY!

UNIT 3

ELEMENT 1

Maintain the equipment

Performance criteria

(a) Equipment within own authority is cleaned as necessary.

(b) Equipment is cleaned according to regulations and with no effect on other users.

(c) Equipment is regularly monitored for wear and faults reported promptly.

(d) Appropriate cleaning materials are identified and used in accordance with regulations.

(e) Equipment diagnostic procedures are carried out regularly to regulations.

(f) All diagnosed faults are reported promptly and with supporting evidence to the appropriate authority.

Range statement

(1) EQUIPMENT Screen, input device, output device.

(2) EQUIPMENT DIAGNOSTICS Automatic, non-automatic.

(3) REGULATIONS Manufacturer's, health and safety, organisation's legislation.

Evidence required

Fault reports produced by the candidate.

Observation of candidate cleaning Information Technology equipment.

Observation of equipment under candidate's authority.

Evidence for this element may come from a realistic working environment.

Questioning is used where necessary to confirm specified knowledge.

Maintain the equipment

The information detailed here covers all the elements necessary for you to successfully complete and attain Unit 3. Some questions or exercises are indicated as we go along and are typed in *italics*.

Try to make notes about each subject covered as you come across it within your college or work placement tasks, so that at the end of the Unit completion of the Competence Statement will not be so time-consuming or difficult. It is often a good idea to have extra copies of the blank forms to hand so that you can jot down the elements you cover as you go and then just rewrite/type your notes for a comprehensive and well documented statement.

This unit is all about the maintenance and care of your equipment. The care of your computer is of paramount importance, if it is to offer you the service that you may require from it. Always ensure that you keep it clean – use the proper cleaning solutions and applicators produced for this job and take any necessary safety precautions as well. Always make sure that before you start cleaning any of the hardware, that the computer is switched OFF! Always follow the manufacturer's guidelines on cleaning each piece of equipment, and remember – **IF IN DOUBT – DON'T!**

Keyboards can become very dirty very quickly, especially if they are used by a number of users on a regular basis – e.g. in a college. Covers are a good idea to keep the everyday dust and dirt out, but can be expensive if large numbers of them are required, or a nuisance if the computers are in regular use and it means constantly taking them off and putting them on again. Never eat or drink in the vicinity of your computer. Accidents can happen and the results can be disastrous not only for yourself, but for the machine as well.

How often do you clean your computer? What solutions do you use and why?

Printers are also sensitive pieces of equipment and may need specialist attention to clean and maintain them so that they can continue to perform efficiently. Never overload a printer with too much paper. This will cause the paper to jam, and it may result in other associated problems. Check the ink cartridges and toner frequently to ensure long-lasting and quality output. Always use the correct cartridges for your printer and never skimp on the cost, as cheap alternatives often result in quicker usage and poorer quality of the printed page. Incorrect ones can also damage the finer mechanisms within the printer itself, which in the long run can cause additional expenditure to put the problem right. Consult the manufacturer's guidelines for detailed information about the care and maintenance of your printer, as well as suitable and recommended consumables to complement it and ensure that it runs smoothly for many years to come.

What type of printer do you use? Can you change the ink cartridges, or is it not part of your job? If not, how would you go about getting a new supply fitted?

Health and Safety regulations again play an important part of the overall care of your computer. You need to be aware of the condition of all your plugs, cables and leads. They need to be checked for fraying and damage. Technicians need to be advised of any problems so that they can deal with them immediately. Broken, loose or damaged keys, damaged floppy disk drives, or just a sticky mouse all need to be remedied so that you can continue to use the computer efficiently. Make sure that you are aware of how to get these problems sorted out.

Unit 3

What procedure do you follow to get assistance with the variety of problems detailed here?

Always be Health and Safety conscious, not only for your own well being, but for those around you as well. Wherever computers are located, make sure that the leads and cables that trail with them are safely out of the way. Coil them up and try to make sure that they do not get into an unholy tangle, or in the way of your feet if under your desk. It is quite easy to catch your foot in a lead whilst sitting at your desk, and to disconnect your keyboard, mouse, printer, or even the power supply – all of which have disastrous consequences for the work that you are doing!

If the cables need to run across the floor, make sure that special protective guards cover them so that as people walk across the office/classroom, they will not trip over them and cause a serious accident. If at all possible try and run them out of harm's way, around the skirting board, or better still have extra and nearer plug sockets fitted so that you avoid extra cabling unless really necessary.

With all the leads associated with a computer and the requirement of plugs as well, it is easy to overload the power supply with too many plugs running off a small adapter. Fit an adapter with the facility to have four or five plugs next to each other. It will also make life easier if you have to disconnect one to find the one that you are looking for. A good idea is also to put a sticky label or 'dymo' tape on each so that you can tell at a glance which one is which, and not disconnect the wrong one by mistake.

Facilities to ensure the continued good 'health' of your computer

Over the years much has been documented about viruses and the problems they can cause. Often they can lie dormant in a system for years just waiting for the appropriate trigger to set them running. They are rogue programs which have been constructed to cause damage to data and information stored in a computer. They cause much damage and everyone needs to be aware of how to prevent the spread of viruses so as to minimise the devastating effects.

Some systems you use often have an automatic virus checker installed, which is activated every time you switch the computer on. This will check all the files and software for any sign of a known virus and will give the all clear if nothing is found. New computer viruses are as prevalent as the latest strain of 'flu, so make sure that your computer doesn't suffer: get the latest virus checker installed, as this will save you a lot of grief in the long run.

Manual checks are also possible once the virus checker has been installed, so that you can check your floppy disks for viruses too. The automatic scan will only check the hard disk and associated software and files stored there. The manual scan checks all the files on the floppy disk and compares the data with virus patterns that it is familiar with and found within the virus checker software. If it detects anything, it will tell you and you then have the option to eradicate the virus from the file/disk using the facilities within the software.

What virus checks are available on the computer that you use? Find out some more about viruses and the damage that they cause. Can you perform a manual scan of a floppy disk from your computer? If not, what procedure do you have to adopt to check it for a virus?

Maintain the equipment

There are many different virus checking packages available which will help your computer to remain 'fit and well' and ready for use. One of the easiest ways to eliminate the possibility of transferring a virus from one computer or system to another is to restrict the use of floppy disks to machines at work/college and not to take them home and use there. Scan each time you use a disk in a different machine, just to be on the safe side.

Often viruses can be transmitted by shareware obtained from the Internet, or by downloading files from there as well. Check your disks, try and keep separate ones for home and work, and always make sure that you do a manual scan on a floppy disk before you use it in another computer to help prevent the risk of infection. If you cannot do this yourself, seek assistance from someone who can. Never underestimate the destruction that a virus can cause!

There are many other diagnostic procedures which can be used to help detect or sort out problems on your computer. You can scan your disk for errors or problems and then utilise solutions to correct them. You can 'defragmentise' your files – in other words put all the pieces together rather than have them located all over the place; this utility will in itself help to make your computer more efficient and help it to function more effectively. (Further information about these facilities can be found in the User's Guide for your computer.)

> *Find out about the other utilities available for you to use on your computer.*

If you experience a major problem with your computer, seek professional help rather than trying to sort it out yourself. You can often cause more damage by doing a self-fix. Your college/workplace may have its own technical department or help-desk facility just waiting to offer you the assistance that you need. Seek their help: after all, it's what they are there for!

Learning to work with others is also a major undertaking and an essential lesson to learn here. Not only do we have to work with each other, but with people above and below us in the hierarchy of the organisation. This also follows if you are a student – you need to work with fellow students, as well as lecturers and any other members of the faculty that you may come into contact with. Listen to what they have to say and if they give you any instructions, or information, follow them precisely. This is especially relevant where computers are concerned. It may be that certain procedures and processes have to be followed, and unless you get them correct, you will not be able to produce the end result successfully.

> *Draw a hierarchical chart of those you work with and your connections with each.*

> *Draw a diagram to detail all your contacts and those you network with regularly.*

Communication with all sorts of people will help you to build up a network of useful contacts: people you can turn to for advice, assistance or just for social conversation. Always seek the authority of your lecturer/superior before you undertake anything which may be outside of your normal working remit. Work within the rules and regulations – they are there for your protection and guidance. Never overstep the mark – always be SAFE in the way that you work!

Unit 3

ELEMENT 2

Maintain data file structures

Performance criteria

(a) Establish data file structures to meet customer requirements in accordance with regulations.

(b) File structure commands are identified and used correctly to create and maintain file structures.

(c) Correct locations are selected for the storage of data files.

(d) File operations within own authority are identified and correctly used.

(e) File structure security requirements are identified and implemented.

(f) Appropriate records maintained are correct and complete.

(g) Media usage and available storage capacity are regularly checked to meet present and anticipated storage requirements.

Range statement

(1) FILE STRUCTURE COMMANDS Move, copy, delete, name, create.

(2) FILE OPERATIONS Storage drive, path, directories.

(3) SECURITY REQUIREMENTS Back-up: frequency, location, media. Access: passwords, identification

(4) RECORDS Back-up log, file structure prints.

Evidence required

Records detailing file locations and structures.

Records of back-ups produced by the candidate.

Observation of the candidate at work over a period of time maintaining data file structures and checking storage capacity.

Evidence for this element may come from a realistic working environment.

Questioning is used where necessary to confirm specified knowledge.

Everyone needs to work methodically whether they are using a manual or a computerised system, so that in the long term this will ensure that work can be easily traced and referred to, rather than having to go through a long process to find the answer to a question or enquiry.

Colleges or organisations will have in place a variety of systems for logging or filing documents manually. Some will be alphabetical, others will be numeric or maybe a mixture of both. It all depends on the category of work being dealt with.

Maintain data file structures

Find some other classifications that can be used for filing systems.

Computer systems need to be treated in the same way so that users can access the information that they need quickly and easily.

The File Manager in Windows 3.1 or Windows Explorer in Windows 95 offer the same sort of facility, just in a different way. For this section we will look in detail at the File Manager facilities as found in Windows 3.1.

Using File Manager

Loading the File Manager

The File Manager is a very useful tool which allows you to organise the files on your floppy disk, or hard drive. This may involve creating backups of files, copying or moving files to other disks or directories, or deleting them, generally whatever is necessary for you to achieve a well organised and effective system for routine and effective 'housekeeping'.

To load the File Manager, you need to have your Program Manager windows displayed and then double click on the *Main* group.

This should then reveal the Main group of icons. If you have done this correctly your screen should look something like the one shown below:

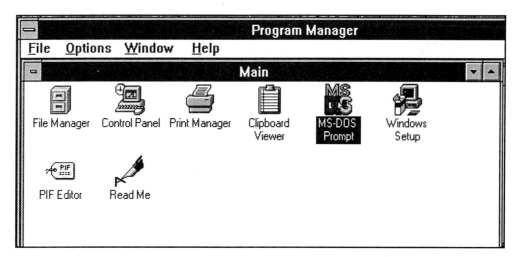

If you cannot find the Main group, then select the Window from the menu bar and choose the option – Arrange Icons. The Main group should then appear. Failing this, ask a tutor or supervisor for assistance.

It is now time to load the File Manager program. This is achieved by double clicking on the File Manager icon which looks like a filing cabinet. (See Using The File Manager in Windows 3.1 in the Appendices at the back of the book, for more detailed instructions about its functions and capabilities.)

When you save a file you need to think of an appropriate name, or to use the house style or naming convention familiar to you. Try to name it so that you will remember what the document is about, or if you use a set format, stick to it. With Windows 3.1 you can only use a maximum of 8 characters before the 3-character file extension. Remember, no spaces or punctuation marks!

Unit 3

Name some of the automatic file extensions that software packages apply to the end of files that you are familiar with.

As previously mentioned, backing up your work onto a floppy disk if you use a network facility, or onto the hard drive on a stand alone PC, will ensure that you have a copy of the file to fall back on if your first one becomes corrupt.

Many organisations implement a routine back-up of all their files. Some files are backed-up on a daily basis, whereas others, perhaps used less, are done on a weekly or monthly basis. Many back-up routines are done during the night when the system is not used. This helps prevent the system from slowing down, or denying access to files as they are backed-up, to users during the day. The data is often stored on magnetic tape, CD-ROM or small cassettes. It is necessary to date and number the medium used so that it can be reinstalled as required should the system crash or a state of emergency occur whereby the data has to be recreated using the back-up files from the previous back-up.

Document your daily, weekly and monthly back-up procedures.

Manual records of all your files and back-ups are often a good idea. This will be able to tell you which files you backed-up and when, also linking these with any numbers that you add to the medium for identification. Keep this information safe so that you will have it available as and when you need it.

Files may be updated by a number of different people for different reasons. Always check that the information you input is accurate and appropriate. Follow any procedures that are in place and work within any time constraints set.

Never do anyone else's work, unless given direct instructions to do so, and never use their password to access their working areas on the computer – this can be construed as a violation of the code of practice laid down by the organisation.

List some of the things that you should not do on your computer. What would be the consequence if you did?

Paper information relating to the work that you undertake may often give an accurate record of how the computer information was input and collated and may even assist in sorting out any problems that may have arisen along the way. Accurate records of who did what and when may hold the key to incorrect or suspect data.

The creation of new files, or databases, can be much simpler if the correct or utilised documentation is to hand so that it is possible to trace the route taken to get to any one point. The requirement for tractability differs from organisation to organisation and often documents have to be kept, by law, for a specified number of years, before they can be archived or disposed of. Never throw a document away, or delete a file, if you think it is important. Check first – it is better to be safe than sorry!

Finally, always make sure that you have sufficient space on your disk or network facility for the safe storage of all your files. Not only the ones that you currently use, the new ones you create, but also any requirements for the future.

If you are thinking about buying a new computer, look ahead and calculate what you will need in the future – will your organisation be twice or three times as big as it is now?

Or

Will you just need a good computer to do your college work on? Give the whole idea some thought, as it is often cheaper to spend more initially than to have to upgrade expensively after only a short period of time because your computer system cannot cope with the work load you are giving it!

Set a realistic budget and then produce a specification for the computer you would like to have to work on at home. Detail why you would need each facility

ELEMENT 3

Maintain media and documentation libraries

Performance criteria

(a) Media and documentation are selected for storage to meet regulations.

(b) Records of type and location of media and documents are maintained correctly and clearly to meet regulations.

(c) Media and documentation updates are correctly carried out as appropriate.

(d) Media and documentation security and copyright requirements are maintained at all times.

(e) Environmental conditions are maintained to regulations.

(f) Redundant media are correctly located and disposed of in line with own authority and regulations.

Range statement

(1) MEDIA Original application software, system software, data.

(2) DOCUMENTATION Manuals, back-up records.

(3) REGULATIONS Manufacturer's software supplier, health and safety, organisation's legislation.

(4) ENVIRONMENTAL CONDITIONS temperature, humidity, light, cleanliness.

Evidence required

Records of library contents.

Updated documentation produced by the candidate.

Observation of the candidate at work over a period of time maintaining libraries.

Observation of libraries under candidates own authority.

Evidence for this element may come from a realistic working environment.

Questioning is used where necessary to confirm specified knowledge.

Unit 3

Documentation is always in abundance either in the workplace or college. New software arrives in the form of floppy disks or CD-ROMs. Both are forms of media, and are usually accompanied by several weighty manuals full of information. These are often written in rather a long-winded and technical form, and do not make easy reading, although the information they contain is very necessary in order to utilise the new software to its fullest potential.

Often these manuals will tell you how to install the software and will illustrate the capabilities of it in tremendous detail. They may also give you ideas on how to resolve problems that may occur and a whole variety of other troubleshooting solutions.

Manuals need to be kept accessible to both users and technicians alike, so that the appropriate information is always to hand. Other forms of media include disks full of data files and other documentation can be thought of as the information you keep on your file structures or as a library of files on different subjects. Company procedures, course information, rules, regulations and policy documents also fall under the category of data or document library information. Employee and student handbooks or charters also fall into the documentation library category.

Make a list of all the documentation that you come into contact with, what it is for and where to find it.

Media – floppy disks, magnetic tape, CD-ROMs and so on – also need to be logged so that it is possible to track down original disks, copies of software or new files. The original software needs to be copied once you obtain it, so that you always have a complete back-up of it should you need to recreate the system at any time. Back-ups of disks need to be logged and stored safely in a fireproof safe or better still off site, so that they are kept safe should there be a fire or other emergency.

Where do you keep your back-up disks and why?

If we consider all the documentation that we come into contact with everyday, we may need to decide which ones one need to keep to hand and those which can be stored safely elsewhere. Making these decisions may be the task of a supervisor, but we too can make similar decisions about our documentation even if it is only for our own home. Take for example all the post that we receive on a daily basis. We all receive a lot of junk mail. What do we do with it? Most of us glance at what it is and either put it on one side to read later or discard it straight away. The principle is the same at work as at home. Some mail we receive we have to deal with immediately – bills or urgent matters, others can be put on hold for a day or two and other items we can safely bin straight away. Some documents need careful reading and deciphering and then filing away for reference at another time. The same applies to manufacturers' information or manuals, licences or other documents received. If we don't deal with them as we go along, there will be resulting problems. Some matters, like our urgent bills, could go undetected and we would get reminders chasing payment.

If manuals or CD-ROMs are used by people outside of the department where they are kept, some sort of logging system needs to be implemented so that everyone will know where they are if they are taken from their usual place. The log should record the date and person who has borrowed them and perhaps a return-by date. Books and software all too easily grow legs and walk if a monitoring system is not put into place early on.

Maintain media and documentation libraries

Copyright also needs to be maintained, as it is often very easy to make a copy of some software to use at home. Software, like books, recordings and manuscripts has its own copyright protection which makes it illegal to copy anything without the prior consent of the author.

Every software package comes with its own licensing agreement. These differ according to the number of users who will be using the application. It can be for a single user, or multiple users. For a specific computer or network, or for a whole site, it all depends on your circumstances and the requirements of the establishment and its users. You will need to predetermine exactly what is required so that you can order the appropriate one along with the software. If you do not have the correct licence for the software, the manufacturer can fine you. These fines are getting heavier all the time in an attempt to stamp out pirate copies and illegal use of software.

What procedures are in place that you know about to prevent the illegal use of software at your college/workplace?

Many organisations utilise a database facility to keep a check on all the software that they use – versions and upgrades, and upon which machine they can be found. Dates of purchase as well as cost and contact names can also be added to give a comprehensive record of all the software purchased and in current use. Sometimes an organisation may pilot a new version of a package, and install it on only a few machines to try it out. Log this as well and also the number of users associated with its licence. It is quite easy to offer it to other users after the conclusion of the pilot scheme, to maintain uniformity throughout an organisation, and then find that you do not have the licences to facilitate this. You will need to remedy this before you start using the software on additional machines that may not be incorporated into the initial licence agreement. Often each department may use a different version of the same package, perhaps different budgets facilitate more expenditure on software than others, or supervisors have different priorities to fulfil. Whatever the reasoning, it is often the case that work is undertaken on a variety of versions of the same package, or even, in the worst scenario, on different packages. Standardisation across the board leads to a more flexible and problem free environment and should be sought as the most advantageous solution to adopt.

List the packages and versions available for you to use on your computer at college/work. Which ones do you use and why?

When a software application upgrades to a new version to facilitate new concepts and functions, you can easily move your already created files from the previous version up to the new version. The software will convert it for you automatically, but you cannot go back down again, there is no facility in the previous version to reconvert the files back again. If you find that this is occurring to the files that you are creating, make sure that once you have moved up a version, you stay there if you can. It will make your work much easier to keep track of, rather than using a combination of several versions of the same software. It will also mean that you can standardise and use the new functions and capabilities that are invariably incorporated into new versions of the software that reach our computers.

Health and Safety, as we have seen before, occurs regularly throughout the whole of this syllabus – try to maintain it at all times as well as being security conscious as well. Stick to the rules. Save your work regularly. Do regular housekeeping to maintain an accurate and up-to-date library of files. Work in a conducive atmosphere, where the conditions are in line with Health and Safety measures.

(More detail about this can be found in the Health and Safety section in the Appendices at the back of the book.)

Suggest ways of improving the way that you work.

Often it needs to be better not harder to achieve an overall end result or objective. Maintain efficient housekeeping procedures – delete redundant or very old files to make room on the system for new ones. Doing this will also make the system more efficient and faster.

Always be security conscious, whether it is related to documentation, software or the organisation/college as a whole. If you are not sure what to do, seek assistance and in doing so avoid a worse possible scenario which may be difficult to get out of without imposing recurring problems on all fronts.

Maintenance embraces computers and equipment in general, documentation, media, software and data – through forethought and appropriate procedures, it is possible to ensure that the system works efficiently and that it will be a joy to use.

CONCLUSION

MAINTAIN THE INFORMATION TECHNOLOGY SOLUTION

Completion of this Unit will demonstrate that you can:
- Competently clean and maintain the computer hardware;
- Undertake appropriate housekeeping operations as a matter of routine;
- Create and maintain file structures;
- Back up files and delete redundant ones;
- Maintain media and documentation libraries.

CONGRATULATIONS – YOU HAVE NOW SUCCESSFULLY COMPLETED UNIT THREE!

To tie up all the loose ends covered in this Unit, try to complete the Unit 3 exercise to produce additional evidence for inclusion in your portfolio.

Maintain media and documentation libraries

EXERCISE

Produce a document to answer the 4 questions/scenarios detailed below which cover the three elements of Unit 3 - Maintain the Equipment, Maintain Data File Structures and Maintain Media and Documentation Libraries.

(1) Obtain the correct cleaning equipment from your supervisor/lecturer and **clean your computer** - screen/monitor, keyboard, mouse and processor unit. Ensure that you have your computer switched off and that you conform to all Health and Safety regulations. Write up what you did and why.

(2) Draw up a check-list of things to do, connected with working with your computer, on a regular basis. Include activities like cleaning, creating/ organising/deleting files and/or directories/folders, organising routine services and maintenance for the hardware, purchasing upgrades of software, renewing licences, ordering consumables, backing-up files to alternative media - daily, weekly, monthly, plus any more that may be essential for you to remember to do. Put them in order of how often they need to be done. Make brief notes or comments as to why you should do each one.

(3) Written documentation or information is vital to support any organisation or system – here is your opportunity to detail what you know and why it is so important.

Imagine that you have to show a temporary person how to use your computer and where to find files etc., which may be required, while you are away on holiday for 3 weeks, getting a tan and a much deserved rest!

Explain any necessary procedures and where to find them documented for reference, which they will have to use: how to log in and out of the system; any passwords necessary to obtain access to various levels of the system for different facilities; where to find supporting documentation and software manuals, Health and Safety procedures and information, contact names and phone numbers. It may also be prudent to detail what to do if a hardware or a software problem occurs, if a virus is detected, if there is a power cut, or if you witness someone abusing or sabotaging the computer system. Where to seek specialist or technical assistance, plus a whole host of other important issues which may need to be addressed before you board the plane, so that you can relax, knowing that the organisation will function smoothly whilst you are away, and the temp will do your job efficiently and effectively.

(4) Give examples of how you have structured your storage media, so you can save files in a logical and easy-to-find manner for use now, and in the future. Also, specify naming conventions used and detail where paper records, if any, of these computer files are kept, should further information be required.

Do you think that it is necessary to keep paper as well as electronic copies? Answer this as your personal/organisational requirements need to be met.

UNIT 4

ELEMENT 1

Contribute to improving the use of information technology

Performance criteria

(a) Facilities which aid effective use and are accurately identified and recorded.

(b) Potential improvements in use are identified and recorded.

(c) Relevant proposals selected are communicated with supporting evidence to appropriate authority promptly.

(d) Resources obtained effectively meet requirements of own work.

(e) Materials are stored safely and securely and are located to provide ready access.

(f) Resources are requested in accordance with organisational procedures.

Range statement

(1) FACILITIES Hardware, software, environment, materials.

(2) RESOURCES Time, materials, hardware, software.

(3) MATERIALS Media, consumables.

Evidence required

Proposals produced by the candidate.

Observation of the candidate at work over a period of time.

Evidence for this element may come from a realistic working environment.

Questioning is used where necessary to confirm specified knowledge.

The information detailed here covers all the elements necessary for you to successfully complete and attain Unit 4. Some questions or exercises are indicated as we go along and are typed in *italics*.

Try to make notes about each subject covered as you come across it within your college or work placement tasks, so that at the end of the Unit completion of the Competence Statement will not be so time-consuming or difficult. It is often a good idea to have extra copies of the blank forms to hand so that you can jot down the elements you cover as you go, and then just rewrite/type your notes for a comprehensive and well documented statement.

Contributions for improving the use of IT within our working or studying world always need to be carefully considered so that we can maximise our potential wherever and whenever possible. Identifying facilities, and whether they are good or bad, is also a way of seeing whether they are effective or not.

> *Look critically at the way you currently work, and how you could perhaps alter it to be more economical on the resources that you use, or more efficient in time allocated to produce the required end result.*

Hardware is often ineffective if it is constantly faulty through lack of maintenance or regular services. Out of date facilities also hinder the effectiveness of the user.

Software also needs to be kept up-to-date so that competitors do not take over and leave you standing. It is also a good idea if all users can operate the same software so that a professional and standard image is achieved company or college wide.

The environment can affect the way that you work. If it is too hot or too cold, if there isn't enough space, or the conditions are generally not suitable for working in, then this too can hinder your work. (See the Health and Safety unit – 5, or the appendix at the back of the book for more detailed information on this subject.)

Materials – disks, paper, print cartridges or toner – and their availability all affect the way in which you work. Sometimes it is easy to use too much of a product, or it is too readily available, or even too easy to steal! Careful monitoring of all products will help to dispense with some of these problems associated with consumable materials that we all take for granted wherever we work or study. Records of all materials used, dates supplied and to whom, can help maintain the effectiveness of the way in which we work with IT related products.

Practical Application:

Produce a table for all the consumable products associated with your college/work place, and complete it on an on-going basis to monitor excessive or regular use. Report back to your tutor or supervisor after a period of regular monitoring of about four weeks and detail what has been happening and why you think the figures may be as they are. Make sure that you record all dates and where the materials have been, or to whom supplied, so that a comprehensive check is possible. (You may need to work in conjunction with others in order to obtain and record the details necessary for this project.)

or

Within all establishments there are procedures for reporting major faults and problems with equipment. Make a note of what they are and how and when to use them. If one particular piece of equipment is continually not working, record the dates and faults separately and then report this problem to your tutor or supervisor so that they can deal with it in the formal manner. Minor faults and problems should be dealt with quickly and efficiently to maintain a continuous working environment. Detail the minor fault reporting procedure in your college/work place. Monitor all faults and record what happens to them. Are there any solutions to long term or recurring problems that you can think of, that will improve the effectiveness of your facility?

If a problem occurs, how do you deal with it? Is there a known procedure which you follow? Reporting problems in the appropriate fashion is a necessary requirement so that they can be followed up and dealt with appropriately. If this is not done, then the facility falls into disarray and does not work effectively or efficiently.

Suggestions for improvements are welcomed in most places, as often the organisations cannot see at first glance what needs to be corrected or improved, whereas you, the user, get a real opportunity to specify exactly what is required to make the task better and you more efficient. This often falls into the category of suggestions for further training on new software to understand and use its facilities better, or to purchase better printers that can print in colour and so produce better quality charts, presentations and graphics to illustrate the work that you, or the organisation as a whole, do. Suggestions and proposals not only benefit you, but can benefit the whole class/college or department/organisation. Some organisations offer a reward for suggestions that are proposed and implemented. This is a good incentive for you to put forward any ideas which you think may benefit everyone, but this should not be the only reason for doing so. The outcome and proposed facility should be sufficient to warrant the proposal.

In order to meet the requirements of your job/course you will also need to utilise a number of resources, the first of these being time. Allocate sufficient time so that deadlines can be achieved. Detail these in your diary or action plan. Record any excess or deficit, and also log the eventual outcome or mark achieved. Sometimes the requirements of the job are specified in an assignment or project brief. Read these carefully and make sure that you can identify all the requirements, as well as envisage the end result. Seek assistance if any resources or requirements are not available, or if the deadlines are too close for comfort. Remember that we all work better with a little pressure applied. Getting the amount right is the trick – too much and we are in overload situation – too little and there is no rush or aim to achieve. If additional resources are required make sure that you apply for them in good time and through the appropriate channels.

Managing materials, like time, is essential and needs to be monitored on an on-going basis. It may be that we have our own personal supply of materials that we need to do the job. If not, then we need to ask for additional ones to be made available to us, or to go and buy what is required, depending on the circumstances. Safe, secure storage of both personal and organisational materials is necessary so that they are not used by other departments/individuals who should not have access to them. They may be part of our allocated and budgeted supply. Security needs to be applied to consumable materials as they often tend to go astray. Careful planning of your future work can help to ascertain your overall requirements and from this you can budget and request appropriate supplies to meet your intended demand.

Practical application:

One suggestion for improving technological facilities, for those of you at college, is the implementation of an e-mail facility for all students. There may already be an e-mail system in place at your college; if not, do some research into suitable packages and associated costs. Make sure that whatever you suggest is appropriate to your hardware facilities and capabilities. Look at who would have to set up the user identities and how this could be achieved. How would you record all the identities? Someone always seems to forget theirs and needs to have it reinstated. Who would do this? Would all staff and students have access to the system, or just those teaching/studying on the relative courses? How would you determine who would have access? Look at the advantages and disadvantages of implementing such a system. How would implementing an e-mail system at college improve or develop your own use of Information Technology?

A possible advantage is that notices would be given to all students at the same time regardless of whether they were absent or not, therefore ensuring that everyone would have the same information, provided that they used the system on a regular basis.

A possible disadvantage is that too much time, space and energy may be spent chatting over the facility when students should be working and tutors teaching!

ELEMENT 2

Improve own use of information technology

Performance criteria

(a) Suggestions for improving own use are evaluated and implemented appropriately.

(b) Appropriate reference materials are selected and used for improving own use.

(c) Development needs are identified and agreed with an appropriate authority.

(d) Development plan devised is agreed with appropriate authority to meet identified needs.

(e) Development undertaken is in line with agreed plan and recorded.

Range statement

(1) REFERENCE MATERIALS Supplied documentation, on-line help, published materials.

Evidence required

Development plans and record of achievement produced by the candidate.

Observation of the candidate at work over a period of time.

Evidence for this element may come from a realistic working environment.

Questioning is used where necessary to confirm specified knowledge.

Unit 4

Developing and improving your own use of Information Technology needs careful thought, consideration and planning.

You need to look carefully at the job that you are doing, or the college course you are attending and analyse how you could improve what you currently do. It may be that you need to enlist professional help with regard to training so that you can undertake more responsibility at work, or use the new software better than you currently do.

College tasks may be different, as you have to develop ways and means to achieve the end result. Time management may fall into this category, especially if you are planning to take professional exams as an addition to this course. A suitable revision timetable may be a good thing to produce so that you can practice and revise well in advance, but at the same time you do not leave out any vital course work necessary for the completion of your NVQ syllabus.

Whatever you decide to do, you will need to liaise with your tutor or supervisor so that you get their agreement and support for the plans that you intend to implement. You need to ensure that whatever you suggest, it is both practical and realistic, and not just wishful thinking. It may be that you have to work within budgetary guidelines. This is especially true if you are planning your project around something that you do at work. It needs to be a project that will be a benefit to everyone directly concerned with the work that you do. For college or course related projects, these need to be realistic and beneficial, as you may need to put a great deal of work into implementing them and you need to see a positive result at the end, in recompense for the time that you have invested.

With simple projects it may just be a case of doing some initial research, or a feasibility study, to justify the time to be spent on the project. With more complex tasks, you may not only need to enlist expert help, but also to consult reports, documents and manuals to support your request. If you do some initial investigation and present your argument including the supporting evidence, and in such a way that it is positive and achievable, then your research will have been justified.

Whatever the task – either simple or complex – be prepared to listen to what others may say in support, or otherwise, of the project. College or course related projects need to be simple but effective in order to be possible within the time constraints and limitations that college life permits. Never venture out on any project without the support and authority of those you work with, as it may otherwise end up in the waste paper basket.

Identify what you think may be a suitable project – e.g. production of an exam timetable (college) or additional training at work, so that current software may be used to its maximum potential. Speak to others to help clarify exactly which is the best way to proceed. Identify the overall aim, and specify a time scale for it to be realised in. Produce an action plan detailing each process and when it is to achieved by. Show any delays and state why they occurred. If an action plan is a bit ambitious, then use a diary format, and log the progress, or otherwise, on a day-by-day or week-by-week entry.

Sometimes you come up with a suitable idea, but others will have had the same idea. Don't be deterred by this. Continue to produce the diary and other documentary evidence that you need, and perhaps at the end of the project compare your results with each other. Look at the different ways you each tackled the same topic and work out the advantages and disadvantages for each.

EXERCISE

College Based – Practical Application:

Produce a table, which will detail all your assignments or past paper exercises that you do in readiness for sitting professional exams. Show all the dates of the papers undertaken, the date you did them, and the mark/grade you achieved. This will be a record of achievement which you can keep in your portfolio of evidence. It will show your progress, and also help you to keep track of which papers you have done, and which ones you still have yet to do.

This is a good exercise in producing tables and keeping running records, both of which are ideal candidates for improving your own use of IT.

Work Based – Practical Application:

Look at your current role and isolate one aspect that you feel needs to be developed – e.g. additional computer based training to utilise the software better. In doing this it may mean that you can produce more comprehensive reports and diagrams, charts etc, or just be able to do your job more efficiently.

or

Get involved with some other members of your team/department and start to produce a monthly or bimonthly newsletter for your department to keep everyone informed and in touch with each other. Log birthdays and special events, meetings and social trips/events. It can be as simple or detailed as you like. Document each meeting and how the group works together. Include draft and original copies in your portfolio and also look at the advantages and disadvantages of implementing a scheme such as this. How would producing a newsletter improve or develop your own use of Information Technology?

A possible advantage is that it keeps everyone in touch, with no excuses for not knowing what is going on.

A possible disadvantage is that it takes up too much time to do at work, with your current heavy workload and therefore encroaches on precious time at home. Plus, it always seems to come down to you to do it all!

Unit 4

ELEMENT 3

Contribute to effective use of information technology

Performance criteria

(a) Tasks are identified and prioritised according to organisational procedures.

(b) Appropriate planning aids are used to schedule work.

(c) Where priorities change, work schedules are adapted accordingly.

(d) Anticipated difficulties in meeting deadlines are promptly reported to the appropriate authority.

(e) Assistance is sought where necessary, to meet specific demands and deadlines.

(f) Wastage of resources is minimised.

(g) Work practice is in accordance with organisation's standards.

Range statement

(1) TASKS Routine, unexpected, important, urgent.

(2) RESOURCES Time, hardware, software, materials, magnetic media, consumables.

(3) PLANNING AIDS Diaries, schedules, action plans.

Evidence required

Plans and schedules produced by the candidate.

Observation of the candidate at work over a period of time.

Evidence for this element must come from a realistic working environment.

Questioning is used where necessary to confirm specified knowledge.

Tasks are often given to you as part of your routine work, or course work, and times and dates are linked to them, e.g. a piece of course work to be handed-in by the following week's class, or a series of letters to be typed in time to catch the 4 o'clock post later that day. Firstly, we need to ascertain the exact requirements about each task, and to confirm deadlines if we are unsure about them. Sometimes it is necessary to reshuffle your current workload, so that these new deadlines are met. Learn how to do this so that everyone concerned benefits, and that no undue pressure is exerted onto either the user or the student. This reprioritising can be a simple or a complex task, it all depends on what other tasks you have underway. If in doubt as to which way to turn, seek guidance from your tutor or supervisor, so that all deadlines are achieved and priorities met.

As we have already discussed, time management is very effective if implemented correctly. Priorities have to be noted and dealt with first. These can be detailed on either a TO DO list, or on an action plan which shows dates that they have to be achieved by. If you are unable to determine the correct priorities for a piece of work, either at college or at work, then you need to seek assistance from your tutor or supervisor, so that the correct priority can be set.

We all try to keep a diary at the start of each New Year, but how often do we put it aside as a waste of time? Sometimes it is crucial to keep track of meetings, course work hand-in dates and other deadlines which loom on the horizon. It is not a case of it being a nicety, but a necessity. Today we can find many different versions of diaries and planners. From those that cover 'a week at a glance', to 'a day per page', right through to wall charts and planners, as well as academic diaries – which run from September to July. Technology offers another solution in the form of electronic diaries, which offer state-of-the-art facilities for keeping track of your commitments and the movements of others at work, at the touch of a button.

Practical Application:

Identify the type of diary most suitable to meet your needs at college/work. What sort is it and why? Investigate the types of electronic diaries that are available on the market. How expensive are they? How efficient and reliable are they? Would one be suitable for you to use?

Having found out as much as you can about them, produce a report to detail the advantages and disadvantages of this facility, and recommend why they should or should not be used at your college/work/work placement.

Looking after the financial aspects of any person/organisation is a real headache, and needs careful monitoring so that excess expenditure does not occur. Resources and consumables are expensive commodities too, and need to be treated with care. When working, either at college or at work/work placement, try not to exceed your allocation of time, paper or any other items that you utilise regularly, otherwise you may find that in the future your allocation may be denied or seriously curtailed.

Hardware and associated resources also need to be looked at with care, to ensure that the most appropriate use is being made of them. Try not to over or under utilise, and always make sure that regular services and maintenance are applied.

Time is another valuable resource, and this too, as we have previously stated, needs careful management. As a result of work overload, you can suffer from stress and a variety of associated illnesses. Too little to do and you kick your heels or waste time in doing things which are not job-related or relevant.

Part of working effectively, either at college or work/work placement, is the successful use of resources and the ability to not waste them. By following company or college guidelines, you will achieve this, and planning your work before you start will help to collect and consolidate your ideas, and then carry them out according to plan. This will also help you to achieve any targets set and to maximise your potential as well as to minimise any wastage of allocated resources.

We all need to be 'green' in today's world, and one way that we can do this is to recycle any paper that we do not need. Some printers will use paper that you have already printed on one side of, others will not. If you can, produce draft copies of

Unit 4

documents on used paper, so as not to waste new sheets. If this is not possible, make sure the paper that is not required is put into a recycling bin so that it can be sent off for recycling. Sometimes the money that this generates can be used to help and support local charities. This is a definite benefit and comes from something as simple as recycling paper.

Find out if you can print on both sides of the paper that you use, in the printers at college/work. If not, how do you recycle your waste paper? Make some suggestions about other ways to reduce the wastage of resources. Collate all this information into a report that you could submit to your college/work place on how to become 'greener' and more efficient.

ELEMENT 4

Establish and maintain working relationships with other colleagues

Performance criteria

(a) Opportunities are taken to discuss work related matters with relevant colleagues.

(b) Essential information is passed to all appropriate colleagues promptly and correctly.

(c) Effective working relationships are maintained with individuals and teams.

(d) Commitments to others are met within agreed timescales.

(e) Changes in agreed timescales are agreed with appropriate authority.

(f) Methods of communication and support used are suited to the needs of other colleagues.

Range statement

(1) COLLEAGUES Line managers, immediate colleagues, other colleagues with work related activities.

(2) OPPORTUNITIES Formal, informal.

(3) COMMUNICATION Oral, written.

Evidence required

Written communications produced by the candidate.

Observation of the candidate at work over a period of time.

Evidence for this element must come from a realistic working environment.

Questioning is used where necessary to confirm specified knowledge.

Establish and maintain working relationships with other colleagues

Teamworking, or working in groups or pairs, plays an important part of any course. Learning how to integrate with each other is probably one of the first things that we learn about at the start of any course.

In this case, we all come together as individuals with a common goal (to attain the final qualification) but currently we maybe working on our own, perhaps a little bewildered and confused by a change in the way of life we find ourselves in. This may be as a result of perhaps returning to study after many years away from the classroom.

As we form into groups, perhaps with others who live near us, have children the same age, or hobbies and ideals of the same value, we begin to form friendships and associations which will be useful to us in the future.

Tuckman was a great provider of information appertaining to interpersonal skills and the forming of groups, both within the educational sphere, as well as in the workplace.

He recognised that there were four major stages in the forming of a group – *forming, storming, norming and performing.*

STAGE 1 – **Forming** – during this stage, the group is just coming together and may still be seen as a collection of individuals, each one wishing to impress his/her personality on the group, while its purpose, composition and organisation are being established.

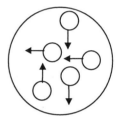

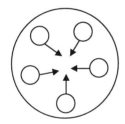

STAGE 2 – **Storming** – the second stage frequently involves more or less open conflict between group members ... If the group is developing successfully, this may be a fruitful phase as more realistic targets are set and trust between the group members increases.

STAGE 3 – **Norming** – this is a period of settling down. There will be agreement about work sharing, individual requirements and expectations of the output.

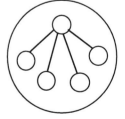

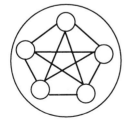

STAGE 4 – **Performing** – once this fourth stage has been reached, the group sets to work to execute its task – this stage marks the point where difficulties of growth and development no longer hinder the group's objectives.[1]

What stage of group formation are you at within your college course, or at work? How have you arrived at this answer?

---

[1] Business Basics – Organisational Behaviour – Various – BPP – 1995

The concept of relationships exists not only within groups of students, but also with the social aspect appertaining to the role of the tutor alongside groups of students. We all can appreciate the impossible task of getting on with everyone. "Group relationships focus on the interaction within and between groups and the stable arrangements that result from such interaction."[2] We always have to realise that everyone is a unique person, and we all have very individual needs and aspirations which it is our task to facilitate during our time of study.

Working relationships may be very different from those that we build whilst with fellow students, but on the whole they follow in much the same vein. We may need to belong to a group at work to ease the workload, or the tedium, or to share resources. Whatever the need, the group forming follows much the same pattern as Tuckman detailed wherever and whatever we are doing.

Meetings and discussions take place within both the classroom and the workplace, and they may need to be technical, constructive or light-hearted, all depending on the subject under discussion. Working in an amicable atmosphere is far better for everyone concerned than one of conflict and anarchy.

Often when groups of people are left to their own devices, they manage to perform very well, but this may depend on the types of people within the grouping itself. Group dynamics is a specialist and often volatile subject. Belbin, a theorist, recognised the fact that a set of characteristics in people needed to be present in the dynamics of a group in order for it to function cohesively. There were eight characteristics and his full set of "Useful People to Have in Teams"[3] includes:

chairman – calm, self-confident, controlled

shaper – highly strung, outgoing, dynamic

plant – individualistic, serious-minded, unorthodox

completer-finisher – painstaking, orderly, conscientious, anxious

company worker – conservative, dutiful, predictable

resource investigator – extroverted, enthusiastic, curious, communicative

monitor-evaluator – sober, unemotional, prudent

team worker – socially orientated, rather mild, sensitive.

Think carefully about you and your role in a group. Which of the above characteristics do you display? What other members of the group can you identify, from studying Belbin's list of Useful People?

We all experience times of stress and problems, either related to our working or home life. No matter how hard we try, we cannot always leave behind the problems that we have, and this often makes us difficult to work with. Some people are naturally difficult, no matter what has happened the day before, and we have to do our best to maintain a good working relationship with them. Other people are no trouble at all,

---

[2] Organisational Behaviour – Andrzej Huckynski & David Buchanan – Prentice Hall 1991
[3] Management Teams – Why They Succeed or Fail – R. M. Belbin – Butterworth-Heinemann 1981

and soon firm friendships develop, which may even give rise to social outings outside of college/work.

In order for a new class of students to learn to integrate with each other, different group exercises may be set to help you learn about each other and your strengths and weaknesses. It is these abilities which will come into play in the future as you progress on the course. Even within the workplace, it is necessary to help new members of the workforce to become a part of the department, and to put them at their ease so that they will work more efficiently and effectively.

Wherever you are based, you will have to learn to work with people who are above and below you in the organisation's hierarchy. These may be supervisors, line managers, department managers or directors within the workplace; or lecturers, heads of schools and even the principal or vice principal. Communication is vital at whatever level and wherever you find yourself. With the best will in the world, most of us are **not** mind readers, and we have to be told what the problem is, or what is expected of us, otherwise we will not know.

In most establishments, there are two forms of communication – formal and informal. Formal is usually what they want you to know, and that which is passed along the organisational hierarchy through a number of mediums – meetings, newsletters, reports, notices and many others. The informal aspect, which normally works alongside the formal one, tends to be based on rumour, supposition, and gossip – in fact, it's the grapevine, or as I once heard – "just tell Dennis!"

Produce a list of all the formal and informal means of communication that you can think of and document their advantages and disadvantages.

Information may be given in various forms – documented or verbal, but mostly it is an instruction. We need to take notice of these instructions and to carry out each element so that a successful end result is achieved.

Seeking help may also be another form of communicating, networking or maintaining an effective working relationship. Often we are left to fend for ourselves, for it is in being independent that we often acquire more information than by being told. This is especially true where computers and new software is concerned. Training classes are a bonus, but first you need to experiment and play in order to understand how, and how not, to do things. The refinements come later on, hopefully in the training programme.

Another aspect that we need to consider within the remit of this element, is to work within given timescales. Often we are given a task, either at college or at work, to produce a piece of work, which has to be handed in, or achieved by a certain time/date. Homework assignments usually fall into this category, and it is essential that we all learn to use our time wisely in order to meet these deadlines. If, for whatever reason, we are unable to achieve the deadline, seek assistance, or an extension, whatever is the more realistic in the circumstance. i.e. – extension to homework hand-in date, or assistance with the workload, so that the post can be caught that day and the urgent mail will be sent out in time.

How would you go about managing your time more effectively?

Unit 4

Time management is an art form and needs careful working on. Initially, you need to organise your work or study load so that you know exactly what has to be done and by when. This may take the form of a simple **TO DO** list with dates by the side of each piece of work. Priority may have to be given to work with shorter deadlines so that they are achieved, and this can be shown by colour coding or putting letters, or numbers, by those things to do first, or just by sorting it into date order.

Produce a suitable TO DO list for college and/or work. Provide a key to explain any codes etc.

We all work better with a certain amount of pressure applied to us, although it has to be determined just how much we can stand before we go into overload situation which can often result in ill-health, and mental or physical stress.

What would you do if you thought that a fellow student/colleague was suffering from stress, as a result of too much to do at college or work?

If you are in a situation at work whereby you can delegate some of the minor tasks to others – do so. Free up some time so that you can do the things that YOU need to do, rather than those things which anyone can do. Spend some time looking at how you can make your day more efficient, and finally, *take some time out to relax.*

ALL WORK AND NO PLAY MAKES JACK/JILL A DULL PERSON!

Seek assistance, as you need to. Never be ashamed to ask for help: it is better to do that than to get into a serious situation which may be more difficult to get out of. Listen to your instructions carefully, and write them down if you think that this may help later on to remember the finer details of the task. If a problem occurs, get all your facts straight. Never invent something to save face.

When working in a group or team, always respect the other members who make it up. Listen to their side of things. Learn by their experiences. Negotiate and compromise as necessary. Never take credit for something that you did not do – you would not like this to happen to you! Be fair and willing to participate and you will find that soon you have made firm friends and many useful contacts as well as the ability to maintain effective working relationships both in college and in the workplace.

CONCLUSION

Monitor the effectiveness of the information technology solution

Completion of this Unit will demonstrate that you can:

- Identify effective and ineffective facilities – hardware, software, environment and materials;
- Come up with ideas on how to improve your own working environment;
- Know what procedures to follow to report major and minor faults and get them repaired;
- Manage your own time and resources effectively, as well as be aware of those resources that need managing organisation-wide;
- Develop personal action plans;
- Manage your time effectively;
- Produce TO DO lists to show priorities and general workloading;
- Plan your work in advance and order/purchase any consumable materials;
- Prioritise your work;
- Reprioritise your work to accommodate additional/urgent tasks;
- Understand the necessity of maintaining a secure and documented facility for the storage of consumable materials;
- Establish and maintain effective working relationships.

CONGRATULATIONS – YOU HAVE NOW SUCCESSFULLY COMPLETED UNIT FOUR!

To tie up all the loose ends covered in this Unit, try to complete the Unit 4 exercise to produce additional evidence for inclusion in your portfolio.

UNIT 5

ELEMENT 1

Monitor and maintain health and safety within the working environment

Performance criteria

(a) Hazards are corrected if within own authority.

(b) Hazards outside own authority are promptly and accurately reported to the appropriate authority.

(c) Actions taken in dealing with emergencies conform to regulations.

(d) Emergencies are reported promptly and recorded correctly, completely and legibly in accordance with regulations.

(e) Working environment which do not conform to regulations are promptly and correctly reported to the appropriate authority.

(f) Working environment is organised to minimise risk to self and others.

Range statement

(1) HAZARDS Faults in main supplies, faults in equipment, obstructions to safe passageways, hazardous cables, unsuitable positioning and use of furniture.

(2) REGULATIONS Manufacturer's, software supplier's, health and safety, organisation's, legislation.

(3) EMERGENCIES Illness, accidents, fire, evacuation.

(4) WORKING ENVIRONMENT All hardware, fixtures and fittings within own area of responsibility, all areas within the organisation.

Evidence required

Reports produced by the candidate.

Observation of the candidate's working environment.

Observation of the candidate at work over a period of time.

Evidence for this element may come from a realistic working environment.

Questioning is used where necessary to confirm specified knowledge.

VIDEO BONANZA

	PRICE PER DAY	DAYS' HIRE	TOTAL COST (B4*C4)	EXTENDED HIRE SPECIAL OFFER PRICE	SAVING	PRICE PER DAY INCREASE OF 10%	SPECIAL OFFER PRICE INCREASE OF 5%
TELETUBBIES	£1.50	66	£99.00	£5.00		£1.65	£5.25
PRETTY WOMAN	£1.00	19	£19.00	£2.50		£1.10	£2.63
ALIEN	£1.00	14	£14.00	£2.50		£1.10	£2.63
DELIA SMITH'S COOKERY CLASS	£1.00	12	£12.00	£2.50		£1.10	£2.63
TWINS	£1.00	12	£12.00	£2.50		£1.10	£2.63
SCRUPLES	£1.00	12	£12.00	£2.50		£1.10	£2.63
AINSLEY'S BARBECUES	£1.00	11	£11.00	£2.50		£1.10	£2.63
DUMBO	£0.50	5	£2.50	£1.00		£0.55	£1.05
STAR TREK - THE FINAL FRONTIER	£1.00	4	£4.00	£2.50		£1.10	£2.63
TOP GUN	£1.00	3	£3.00	£2.50	£0.50	£1.10	£2.63
LETHAL WEAPON	£1.00	3	£3.00	£2.50	£0.50	£1.10	£2.63
CAN'T COOK WON'T COOK	£1.00	3	£3.00	£2.50	£0.50	£1.10	£2.63
STAR WARS - TRILOGY	£1.00	3	£3.00	£2.50	£0.50	£1.10	£2.63
K9	£1.00	3	£3.00	£2.50	£0.50	£1.10	£2.63
BARNEY AND FRIENDS	£0.50	3	£1.50	£1.00	£0.50	£0.55	£1.05
WINNIE THE POOH AND FRIENDS	£0.50	3	£1.50	£1.00	£0.50	£0.55	£1.05
LIVE AND LET DIE	£1.00	2	£2.00	£2.50		£1.10	£2.63
GOLDFINGER	£1.00	2	£2.00	£2.50		£1.10	£2.63
TURNER AND HOOCH	£1.00	2	£2.00	£2.50		£1.10	£2.63
BEETHOVEN	£1.00	1	£1.00	£2.50		£1.10	£2.63

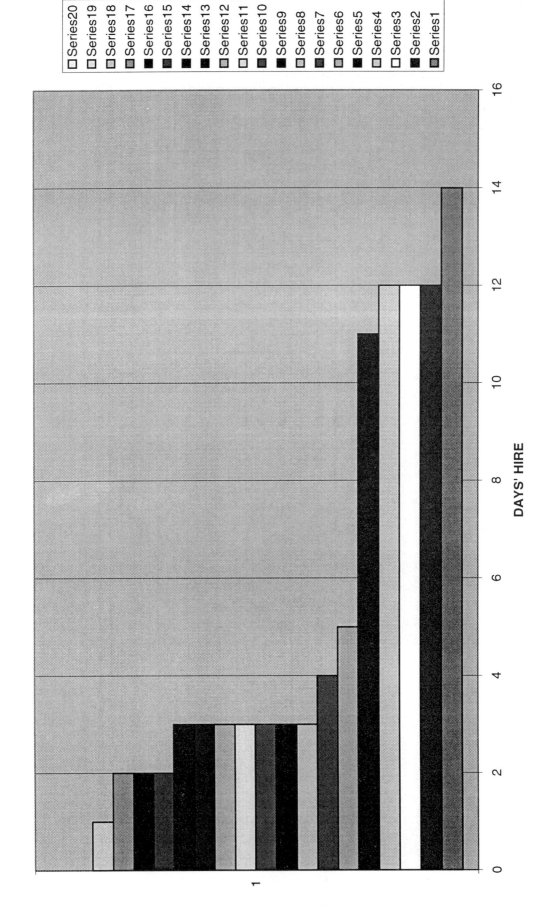

GRAPH OF TITLES BY POPULARITY

VIDEO BONANZA

Good news everyone, videos are now **EXTRA CHEAP** to rent, which is especially good news as the Easter Holidays are nearly with us again, and it is never easy to keep the children amused when the weather is uncertain!

Well here's the answer!

Rent a selection of videos to keep them entertained at special offer prices, and they will be happy for hours. Over the page is a graph which highlights our top twenty titles – there are plenty of others to choose from too.   SEE YOU SOON.

VIDEO BONANZA

TITLES 1 - 20

DAYS' HIRE

Series 1: TELETUBBIES
Series 2: PRETTY WOMAN
Series 3: ALIEN
Series 4: SCRUPLES
Series 5: TWINS
Series 6: DELIA SMITH'S COOKERY CLASS
Series 7: AINSLEY'S BARBECUES
Series 8: DUMBO
Series 9: STAR TREK - THE FINAL FRONTIER
Series 10: WINNIE THE POOH AND FRIENDS
Series 11: BARNEY AND FRIENDS
Series 12: K9
Series 13: STAR WARS - TRILOGY
Series 14: CAN'T COOK WON'T COOK
Series 15: LETHAL WEAPON
Series 16: TOP GUN
Series 17: TURNER AND HOOCH
Series 18: GOLDFINGER
Series 19: LIVE AND LET DIE
Series 20: BEETHOVEN

UNIT 7

ELEMENT 1

Enter data to create and update images

Performance criteria

(a) Authority to access files and images is obtained as necessary.

(b) Sources of files and images required are correctly identified and located.

(c) Images are entered completely using appropriate input device correctly and to schedule.

(d) Files saved conform to organisation's agreed standards.

Range statement

(1) FILE New, existing.

(2) IMAGES Bitmap, vector.

(3) INPUT DEVICE Keyboard, selection device, scanner.

(4) ORGANISATION'S STANDARDS Naming convention, location, frequency.

Evidence required

Vector and bitmap images entered by the candidate.

Observation of the candidate at work over a period of time entering images.

Evidence for this element may come from a realistic working environment.

Questioning is used where necessary to confirm specified knowledge.

The information detailed here covers all the elements necessary for you to successfully complete and attain Unit 7. Some questions or exercises are indicated as we go along and are typed in *italics*.

Try to make notes about each subject covered as you come across it within your college or work placement tasks, so that at the end of the Unit, completion of the Competence Statement will not be so time-consuming or difficult. It is often a good idea to have extra copies of the blank forms to hand so that you can jot down the elements you cover as you go, and then just rewrite/type your notes for a comprehensive and well documented statement.

Enter data to create and update images

Like most of the files/documents we have been dealing with, you always need to obtain the appropriate authority before you utilise an existing file, if it is not your own. Check the filename and make sure that you select the correct one, once authority has been granted.

Tasks are often given as a completely new job, and if so, this is a case of starting from scratch. When this occurs, make sure that you completely understand all the requirements, and that you feel confident to complete the task within the given timescale. If there appears to be a problem, sort it out sooner rather than later. Seek the advice and assist-ance of the customer concerned, or speak to your supervisor for his input on the subject.

Some existing files are stored in different locations, and often these are accessed through a variety of levels of passwords. These levels protect the data and information that is stored there. If you are given the authority to access them direct, and are trusted with the appropriate passwords, do not write them down, or divulge them to anyone else. The maintenance and security of the data and the integrity of the system is vital at all times, and it is easy to neglect the safety of the data by leaving the passwords around for others to see and use.

Once you are totally sure of the requirements, and exactly what you have to produce and by when, you can proceed to load up an appropriate software package for the task in hand.

What software can and do you use, and why?

If you do not have a full-blown desktop publishing or graphics package available to use, you can still produce a wide variety of documents and graphics by using the clip art facility in many word-processing packages.

To be able to use the facilities to their best advantage, a number of input devices are available to use. The most popular are the keyboard and mouse, but nowadays scanners are used extensively to input images, photographs and text into computer format. Lightpens and trackballs are also used, but have more specific uses than the keyboard and mouse. Lightpens offer greater control when dealing with complex and technical images, and trackballs are usually found on laptop computers.

What sort of input device do you use, and why? Do you have access to a scanner? If so, scan in a photograph, a graphic image and a piece of text. Produce three separate documents for inclusion in your portfolio of evidence. If you do not have access to a scanner, find out about the different types of scanners available, cost and capabilities.

Save any work that you produce to the correct location and using the appropriate naming convention. Print out any documents you have produced, and make sure that they do not contain confidential or sensitive material. If they do, write about how you created and produced them, and perhaps illustrate this information with copies of the graphic you used, omitting the sensitive areas, thus demonstrating your ability to utilise graphics confidently and competently.

Unit 7

There are two main sorts of graphic image, and these are VECTOR GRAPHICS and BITMAP IMAGES.

Vector graphics are made up of lines and will be used mainly to construct precise and complex images, technical drawings and other images created by, for example, the drawing office. They are often constructed using specialist packages and high powered and very expensive computer-aided-design (CAD) equipment. CAD systems also offer a rotational aspect or view on screen, so that the user can see all around the image. This can also be thought of as a 3D (three-dimensional) image. Computer games use this type of vector graphic image for the graphics that they contain. As many of you will no doubt know, the quality of computer games has developed drastically over the past ten or twelve years: they are far superior and more complex than they were originally.

Bitmap images basically consist of blocks or colour, and the majority of packages use this form today. Clip art and graphic images, contained in software, are effectively used to produce professional documents and to enhance their general production: these too are bitmap images.

Bitmap images can be reshaped, resized and recoloured according to your personal requirements. You should always remember to take care when reshaping or resizing, as it is easy to distort the image, and it will not look as good as it did before you started altering it.

There are many graphics packages available to help you to produce excellent graphics, as well as a vast number of desktop publishing and presentation products. Look at your requirement before investing in any software, and ascertain if it will give you the freedom you need, and also that it will accomplish 99% of the tasks that you are required to undertake.

Copyright is an another aspect that needs to be considered here. Always read the small print on any licensing agreement, and also reread Unit 5.3 for further detailed information on the subject.

ELEMENT 2

Produce required graphical image by manipulating data

Performance criteria

(a) Customer graphical image requirements are accurately established, verified and checked.

(b) Options for graphical image are identified, and preferred solution agreed with customer.

(c) Facilities to enter, select and combine stored images are correctly used to meet requirements.

(d) Facilities are selected and used correctly to manipulate image.

(e) Facilities to create additional elements are used correctly to meet requirements.

(f) Facilities to alter attributes are used correctly to meet requirements.

(g) Graphical image is checked to be complete and to meet customer requirements.

Range statement

(1) FACILITIES Size, location, orientation, rotation, invert.

(2) ATTRIBUTES Colour, shade, patterns, size, shape.

(3) ADDITIONAL ELEMENTS Line, shape, text.

Evidence required

Three graphical images produced, covering the range.

Details of customer requirements.

Observation of the candidate at work over a period of time establishing customer requirements for a graphical image.

Evidence for this element may come from a realistic working environment.

Questioning is used where necessary to confirm specified knowledge.

Manipulating data, as we have discussed before, gives you the ability to update an existing file. Choose one that will be appropriate for this element and make sure that it doesn't matter if you change its format. If you have been given a specific task for this element, then so much the better; if not, design a suitable document for yourself.

Unit 7

Practical Application and UNIT 7 - EXERCISE:

Select your document, either in agreement with your customer or supervisor, or through your own choice, as a suitable file for this exercise.

Firstly, print out a copy of the document, if it is an existing one, so that you have a 'before and after' image to refer to.

Next, change the page orientation from landscape to portrait, or vice versa. Decrease or increase the margins around all the sides so that the overall size changes. Select one of the graphics contained within its structure – it should now appear with black handles on all the way round, and reshape and resize it, by dragging on any one of these handles. This will now have totally changed both the page orientation, layout and graphic on the page.

Returning to the graphic, select it again and move its position on the page. Next, change its colour. Add other suitable graphics to complement the context of the document and print out the whole document in its revised format.

If you do not have a suitable existing document to use for this exercise, create one using the following:

Open a new document in either a word-processing package or graphics application, and with the page in portrait layout, design a page which will include both text and graphics. A poster is an ideal choice as this gives you ample opportunity to combine the two requirements on the one page, and in an interesting format.

Input appropriate text in a suitable font; change the size and typeface accordingly. Choose colours if you have a colour printer; if not, patterns or shading to make the images bold and eye-catching. Resize it as required and add further text or images to fill the page. The combination of text and images works well.

Check for any obvious errors and then print out your finished poster. Combine this with a detailed explanation of how you achieved it, and include it in your portfolio of evidence. Also include any additional material or information that was given to you as part of a predetermined task. Highlight, in the explanation, any areas of difficulty, and also those aspects which you manipulated, changed, created and also combined together to achieve the end result.

Unit 7

ELEMENT 3

Output specified image to destination

Performance criteria

(a) Appropriate destination is correctly selected.

(b) The destination device is checked to ensure that it is able to receive output.

(c) Image is verified to be complete and correct prior to output.

(d) Output parameters are identified and set up correctly to meet customer requirements.

(e) Image is sent to correct destination.

(f) Output is checked to be complete and meets the customer's requirements.

Range statement

(1) DESTINATION Local, remote.

(2) DESTINATION DEVICE Hard copy, magnetic storage.

(3) OUTPUT PARAMETERS Page range, number of copies, colour.

Evidence required

Output of three graphical images, covering the range.

Details of customer requirements.

Observation of the candidate at work over a period of time producing required output.

Evidence for this element may come from a realistic working environment.

Questioning is used where necessary to confirm specified knowledge.

(This information is much the same as for Unit 6.4, as both these units deal with sending specific images to a printer, or destination.)

Printing your graphic image or document after you have checked all the data is the final stage. If you are fortunate enough to have a colour printer, then so much the better as the colours will add an extra dimension to the graphical representation.

Before you set the printer running, there are a few checks that you need to undertake so that you do not waste paper and the end result is of a high standard.

First, make sure that the printer is switched on and that it is ready to receive your data – this is called being ON LINE. Another thing to check is the ink/toner – make sure there is sufficient for your whole print run. If you have to find someone to change the cartridge or replace the toner, you will need to restart your print from the required page.

Output specified image to destination

What sort of ink/toner does your printer use? Can you change the cartridge yourself, or do you have to get a technician/supervisor to do it for you?

Paper is another factor worth checking. Make sure there is plenty available, and that it is the type that you require. Graphics are usually printed on plain paper and not headed paper, unless for a special reason. Check the printer trays and send the print via the plain paper tray, or refill the upper or single tray with plain paper. Don't overfill it, or the printer will jam.

What sort of paper does your printer use? Which tray does it use, if there is more than one available?

If your printer experiences a problem, try and sort it out, or get someone who can. Never try and clear the problem by switching it off and on again. We are all tempted to do this, but it can and does cause bigger problems later on. It can also lose work that is already in the buffer and waiting to be printed.

What do you do when your printer develops a fault? Detail the procedure you follow and why it is important to do so.

Planning and forethought will help to eliminate many problems associated with printing and the output of your documents.

We discussed the use of T-switches in Unit 2.3. Reread this to confirm what you may need to know about how to utilise them successfully. Manuals and User Guides are also vital books to have to hand as they will often guide you through some of the problems that you may incur, and also how to use the machine correctly. Treat them with respect, as they are a delicate piece of hardware and can easily go wrong. They need regular servicing and maintenance to prolong their life. With this, and the use of the correct ink/toner and appropriate paper, it will work reliably for you for many hours at a time. Always check the paper type first, as many printers will not produce quality output if substandard paper is used. Look after them, and they will run trouble free for many years and produce reliable and professional documents for you.

Sometimes large and complex graphic images are printed remotely, rather than tying up a small local printer for ages, or they can even be plotted. Plotting gives a much finer and more accurate final image, and is used extensively for large technical drawings, and other computer-aided-design drawings and images. It also offers the possibility of printing on a much larger scale, which is often beneficial for scaled-up and down drawings. Sizes range from A0 to A1.

Find out all about plotters, costs and capabilities. Does your organisation have a plotter? If so, what does it print and why?

Always save your work regularly and to the correct location, using the appropriate naming convention. If you are printing remotely, make sure that the connection between computer and printer/plotter is in place, otherwise save the file to a suitable floppy disk or network facility which you will be able to access from another computer. By saving the file to disk, you are then able to utilise it nearer the location of the plotter, or other suitable printer. Floppy disks are portable, and providing that the other computer has the appropriate software loaded, access is quick and easy. Similarly, if you save it to a net-work facility, access it again at the computer linked into the plotter, and away you go. Always check first that you are not jumping a queue, as often these large printers and plotters get very busy with long-winded jobs, so be prepared to wait. I assure you that the end result will be stunning!

Unit 7

CONCLUSION

Produce graphical images using information technology solution

Completion of this Unit will demonstrate that you can:

- Access suitable software for producing graphics and images;
- Understand appropriate copyright legislation;
- Create and update graphic images using a variety of different software packages and facilities;
- Rotate, resize, reshape, recolour, invert and add suitable attributes to an existing or created image or graphic;
- Sort out any problems associated with using graphics;
- Print the final version to a printer or plotter;
- Save the files to floppy disk or network facility for printing locally or remotely.

CONGRATULATIONS – YOU HAVE NOW SUCCESSFULLY COMPLETED UNIT SEVEN!

To tie up all the loose ends covered in this Unit, try to complete the Unit 7 exercise to produce additional evidence for inclusion in your portfolio.

UNIT 8

ELEMENT 1

Transmit messages using information technology

Performance criteria

(a) Appropriate facilities for transmitting messages are selected.

(b) Messages to be transmitted are checked for completeness and accuracy prior to transmission.

(c) Appropriate transmission parameters are correctly entered.

(d) Messages are transmitted correctly, completely and to regulations.

Range statement

(1) FACILITIES Electronic mail, bulletin boards, facsimile.

(2) TRANSMISSION PARAMETERS Name, reference address, number of copies.

(3) REGULATIONS Organisation's, legislation, equipment manufacturer's, software supplier's, health and safety.

Evidence required

Observation of the candidate at work over a period of time using two different transmission facilities.

Evidence for this element may come from a realistic working environment.

Questioning is used where necessary to confirm specified knowledge.

The information detailed here covers all the elements necessary for you to successfully complete and attain Unit 8. Some questions or exercises are indicated as we go along and are typed in *italics*.

Try to make notes about each subject covered as you come across it within your college or work placement tasks, so that at the end of the Unit, completion of the Competence Statement will not be so time consuming or difficult. It is often a good idea to have extra copies of the blank forms to hand so that you can jot down the elements you cover as you go, and then just rewrite/type your notes for a comprehensive and well documented statement.

Transmit messages using information technology

Today, communication is an essential aspect of our working lives, and it takes a variety of forms. We can communicate verbally – face to face, or over the phone. We can send each other memos, letters, reports and other documents through the internal or external mail system. Similarly, we can send written information by electronic means by using a facsimile (fax) machine, or a computer and e-mail.

This element looks at transmitting messages, i.e. *sending* them to others. We can use either a fax or e-mail facility for this.

Facsimile Machines (FAX)

Fax machines are mostly thought of as stand-alone machines, and for the purpose of this element we need to disregard these because, although they are a means of communication, they do not fall into the electronic communication aspect that we are to consider here.

When you send a fax, it is instant. All you need is the address of the recipient: key this in, press SEND and away it goes! Most organisations have fax machines, so it is likely that you will be able to send documents and information to almost all of them. Directories containing fax numbers are also published, so looking up a number is relatively easy. Costs are comparatively low, and you do know that the information goes directly there, and will not get lost in the post.

Many fax machines use ordinary photocopy paper, so again the cost is at a minimum. Do, however, take care not to overload them as they easily jam up and then no one will be able to get through.

Integral faxes offer exactly the same facilities as stand-alone ones, but they are part of your computer, thus keeping extra equipment to a minimum. This is ideal for a small workstation, or office. It does, however, mean that you have to have a dedicated phone line to facilitate the link, but this is most commonly utilised for access to the Internet and e-mail as well, so it has a multi-function and will justify initial expenditure.

Whatever type of fax machine you have, you will need to make sure that you can operate it correctly. Always include a front cover with your document, so that the receiver knows who it is for, how many pages it contains in total, and who to contact if it comes through illegibly, as is sometimes the case.

> *What sort of fax do you use? Does it use ordinary cut A4 paper, or special fax rolls? Do you use a standard front sheet, or just make up one when you need to? Include a copy of your front sheet, as well as a fax that you have transmitted to someone. Highlight the address/number it is going to, your name and number, as well as the number of pages sent. You may also get a transmission report after you have successfully sent a fax: include this as well. If you do not have a standard front sheet to use, design a suitable one and include it here as well.*
>
> *Also, obtain some information about other types of fax machine, especially if the one you use is a stand-alone. Obtain the necessary details about an integral one. Costs, capabilities and facilities are also useful here.*

The cost of sending a fax is incurred by the length of time that it takes to send the information down the telephone line. The quicker it goes, the cheaper it is. Graphics take longer to send, so the price increases. Similarly, a page full of text, with very little 'white space', will take longer to send.

Faxes, like e-mail, come into their own when there is a postal strike, as they enable communication to continue electronically regardless of the external facilities that are available.

Transmission reports are produced after each transmission sent, or if preferred, these can be produced after a quantity of faxes have been sent. They offer the sender the opportunity to check the fax number used, yet again, and to see whether or not the fax was sent at the first time of trying, or if it had to wait until the line was free, and if so, if it was transmitted in full, or if there was a problem with transmission. Error numbers may be recorded on this report for the sender to pick up on and understand fully the nature of the problem that occurred. It is often easier to write the number '3' instead of:

> **The line was busy, so tried again later, but then I couldn't transmit in full as their machine ran out of paper!!!**

Electronic Mail (e-mail)

This is a method of electronic communication between computers that are linked together. They can be linked by a LAN – local area network. A LAN is a link that runs between departments, rooms, offices, buildings or sites next to each other. For links further afield, you have to utilise either telephone lines or a WAN – wide area network. Some e-mail packages that are connected to a WAN will be able to link up globally. This is especially useful for communication between colleagues for business or pleasure, or for the more serious facility of conducting business quickly and easily. It is possible to pass orders onto suppliers from customers, and vice versa – this is all possible through the use of Electronic Data Interchange (EDI).

To use e-mail, you need to have an address or mail box: what it is called depends on the type of system in use. An address is just like your postal address. Friends and relatives need to know it to send you letters, just as the postman needs to know it to deliver your letters. When other users know your e-mail address, they can send you mail electronically.

With most e-mail facilities it is possible to send documents and attachments along with your message. This is great for important documents that you want to get to someone prior to a meeting, and it may take a while in the post!

Most e-mail systems are quick and easy to use, and in many organisations it has taken over from traditional paper memos and letters. It has been known to improve all levels of communication, and even more so when it is implemented with a training session, so that the users get to understand, first-hand, its capabilities and how to use it efficiently.

One of the first things to learn is to re-read your message before you send it, as it is often too late to recall it once you have pressed the SEND button, and you can look foolish if there are errors in the text, or worse still if you send it to the wrong person by mistyping the address

One of the main advantages of using e-mail is that you can read the information as soon as you receive it, which often is instantaneous. Timing may depend on the distance that the message is travelling. You can add notes onto the end of a received e-mail and send the whole lot back again to the sender – all at the touch of a button. However, although your message is transmitted and received in an instant, there is no guarantee that the receiver will actually read it there and then. They may be in a meeting, on holiday or off sick, and will not be able to read their new mail until they return to their desk.

There are many shortcuts to using some e-mail systems, and as you become a more experienced user, you will become aware of these.

> *Do you use e-mail? If so, what is it called? How often do you read your messages? How do you know if you have any? Can you print out your messages direct from the screen – or via a word-processing package?*
>
> *Investigate the concept of transmitting messages via e-mail, and write a brief report on its associated advantages and disadvantages.*

Sending messages via e-mail to a number of people is also simple. It may be that you have compiled lists of people who perhaps go to the same meetings and therefore need to have copies of the documents sent to them in advance, or people who work in the same department. You can, of course, also distribute to everyone at the same time; this usually comes under the heading of ALL, and is used for general and informal broadcasts or a personal message, but make sure you really want it to go to everyone first!

'DRINKS ARE ON ME AT LUNCHTIME – SEE YOU AT THE PUB!'

Always read all your messages: they may contain useful, important or even urgent information. Also check and make sure that all the information is readable. Typing mistakes can often detract or confuse a vital point, or even distort the whole context of the message.

Regular users of e-mail have developed their own language and abbreviations to speed up their keying-in. There is also a code of conduct which they abide by; it is also utilised on the Bulletin Board facility that we shall be looking at shortly.

This code of practice is called 'NETIQUETTE'. Basically, it suggests that you do not type in capital letters as this gives the impression of shouting. If you want to *emphasise* a word, place it between asterisks, and so on.

> *Find out more about NETIQUETTE.*

The process of speeding up the keying-in takes place through the use of acronyms, or three letter acronyms – TLAs, and some examples of these are:

        BTW – by the way

        FYI – for your information

        KISS – keep it simple, stupid

There are many others which are used regularly, find some out for yourselves.

Another way that has developed to show feeling electronically is through the use of 'emoticons'. These are usually in the format of shapes and symbols which are placed in the written text to show how a user is feeling, or to add depth of feeling to the message.

$:-)$ or $:)$ fun or amusement

$:-($ or $:($ sad or disappointed

$;-)$ winking – believe it if you will!

The general term which refers to these graphic displays within the written text is 'smileys.' $:-)$

Never use the e-mail facility to send angry messages, especially if using the e-mail or Bulletin Board facilities on the Internet. Angry messages are referred to as a 'flame', and if sent to a group of people, can result in 'flame war', so be careful what you write, and more so HOW you write it. Check and double check the contents of your message. Think of the tone in which it is written, and how it will be received. Also, give some thought to your heading or title, as many users who receive mountains of mail may skip boring-looking messages and read only what they feel is interesting by the sound of the title.

PAUL AND MARY TAKE THE PLUNGE

or

BIRTHS, DEATHS AND MARRIAGES

To end your e-mail message, you need to add a 'signature'. This is a piece of text which you add onto the end of your messages, and which contains information about you, the sender. It may contain your name, company name, phone number, e-mail address, and any other information which may be essential. Most 'signatures' should be between four and seven lines long: any longer and it can take over the message!

Bulletin Board Services (BBS)

This facility is similar to e-mail, but it is usually linked to a Service Provider as an additional facility for their subscribers, or a large organisation which has implemented this facility for themselves. Bulletin Boards or BBSs allow users to exchange information and interact with each other. Some e-mail systems give you the option to interact, but BBSs tend to have the monopoly over them for this facility.

BBSs also have the upper hand when it comes to linking and communication on a global scale. Large international organisations which work around the globe may utilise this facility extensively, especially if there is a major project underway. It may be that one part is being manufactured in the States, another in Germany, and it is all being assembled in the UK. Communication is vital, and much time is spent by personnel commuting between countries, if they are not holding videoconferences.

Minutes of meetings need to be sent to *all* interested parties in the project, and one way to do this is to post them onto a BBS. Everyone involved with the project will know of its existence and location, plus any passwords which may be necessary to protect the information stored there. Once the meeting has been held, the minutes are typed up and posted onto the BBS. When the personnel arrive for work at each associated site, internationally, they access the BBS, and find there the information they need from the last meeting. The BBS allows them the opportunity to add notes and amendments to the text, usually in italics, capital letters, or a different font, so as to differentiate who it is from, and it is returned to the sender, updated. This is much quicker than sending the minutes by fax, as nothing can be added to this without retyping it; or by post, as it can take several days for mail to get around the world.

You need to check your BBS regularly to see if any additional information has been received or updated. It is not an efficient facility if you do not do this.

Most BBS facilities are simple to use, although there is always some element of risk when posting information to a facility such as this. Make sure that it is well password-protected, and that only users who need to use the facility know of its whereabouts and existence. That way, you can minimise the risk as much as possible.

Delete old files, and only keep what is current on the system otherwise it will become overloaded, but always take a copy of the transmissions for future reference because once a file has been deleted, it cannot be retrieved.

Copies of appropriate data taken from the BBS can be easily copied again and distributed to interested parties, and careful and continued use of the system will offer realistic and efficient facilities to those who use it.

BBSs that Service Providers offer, facilitate the same type of capabilities, but for subscribers only, as a general notice board for those with a common interest or hobby: a place where they can exchange views, ideals and ideas, and a rare opportunity to interact with each other on a world-wide scale.

Electronic technology has grown enormously over the last decade, especially where transmission and communication are concerned. It is now faster and works globally as well. As the old proverb says:

"The world's my oyster"

I wonder what they would have said if they had known what we know today!

Unit 8

ELEMENT 2

RECEIVE MESSAGES USING INFORMATION TECHNOLOGY

Performance criteria

(a) Appropriate facilities for receiving messages are correctly selected and made ready.

(b) Appropriate location is regularly checked for messages.

(c) Messages received are checked for completeness and accuracy.

(d) Messages received in error are referred to appropriate authority.

(e) Messages are correctly processed to regulations.

Range statement

(1) FACILITIES Electronic mail, bulletin boards, facsimile.

(2) MESSAGES Structured, unstructured.

(3) APPROPRIATE AUTHORITY Sender, line manager, supervisor.

(4) REGULATIONS Organisation's, legislation, equipment manufacturer's, software supplier's, health and safety.

Evidence required

Two messages received using two different facilities.

Observation of the candidate at work over a period of time using receiving equipment.

Evidence for this element may come from a realistic working environment.

Questioning is used where necessary to confirm specified knowledge.

Receiving messages electronically, using either fax or e-mail, means that you have to have your system constantly ready to receive any input. The printer connected to the system also needs to have a constant supply of paper, so that it too can print out any fax messages that it receives. Depending upon how the computer has been configured and set up, it does not have to be switched on for it to receive incoming messages. With e-mail, it will receive them automatically and log them in your mailbox ready for you to read when you next start up your computer.

BBSs are slightly different: they are a facility provided as an additional service to subscribers, and normally to receive messages via this medium your computer has to be switched on.

Always check your system regularly for messages. Some systems play music when a new message is received, others have an icon of an envelope which opens to reveal a slip of paper. This signifies that a new message has been received.

Receive messages using information technology

What happens when you get a new message? If nothing happens to prompt you that you may have a new message, get into the habit of checking your mailbox, at least twice a day. Do you use your e-mail facility regularly? If so, what do you use it for? What are the advantages and disadvantages of this? Some messages often contain confidential material: be aware of this, and know how to deal with them appropriately, using company procedures.

Some e-mail packages often show you which messages you have read, and which are new ones, by a * star, or other symbol next to them, or they may appear as bold on the screen, or highlighted in some other way, so that the user can easily differentiate between old and new mail.

Most mail box facilities have a maximum capacity of messages that they can hold. You need to make sure that you delete any old or unimportant messages on a regular basis so that you always have plenty of room to receive new messages. If you keep too much in your mailbox, new messages won't be able to get through to you, and you may miss out on some important messages.

BBSs usually store all their information in a central location which all users or subscribers know about, so that they can readily access the information they need. A simple screen message may be sent to all interested parties to show them that new information has been received on the BBS, so that they know to access it at their earliest convenience. Again, much depends on the type of system and the facilities it utilises as to the way you receive your messages.

Some messages that are received follow a structured approach – in a direct response to a personal message they themselves received. Others may be more unstructured and available for everyone to read with no specific recipient named. The unstructured approach is the most common one utilised on BBSs – it is more of a general information service, whereas e-mail is named and specific, although of course messages can be sent and received by anyone (see 8.1 for more details on this).

Messages can be received in error – the wrong address used, or a simple typing error. If it looks important when you read it, but it has nothing to do with you, seek advice from your supervisor, or contact the sender direct for assistance on what they want you to do. Whatever action you take, always follow company procedures – it is better to be safe than sorry!

Messages that you receive may be sent to you so that you can forward printed information onto others who do not have an e-mail facility themselves. Print out the message you have received on their behalf, and forward it to the appropriate person as requested.

Paper copies of messages received are a good way of keeping track of important messages, and will help not to clutter up the system unnecessarily. Keep your mailbox accessible because when it is full you will be unable to receive new messages. Often, it is useful to be able to keep track of important information that you have received and also it may be necessary to substantiate any actions that you took as a result of a message received. If you delete the message from your mail box, then there is no trace or evidence left to substantiate your actions, but if you have paper proof, then it will be readily available, and may just get you out of deep water!

The main disadvantage of an e-mail facility is that you cannot sign any documents that you send, so the receiver has no proof of authentication. Anyone could have sent it! We looked at signatures in 8.1, but it is quite easy to replicate another person's if you have half a mind to. Some users have a special symbol that they use to authenticate what they send, so that the recipient knows that it is genuine.

How do you know if what you receive on e-mail is genuine or not? What would you like to see done to assist with this problem? What other disadvantages are there with the system that you use? Produce a document to highlight these, plus any other information that you feel would be of value to other users, and in particular recipients of e-mail, via a similar system.

On the other hand, e-mail is a very flexible service, and is especially useful for people who travel around, as it is possible for them to access their mailbox using a laptop or other computer system. They type in their access code and can then look into their mailbox and see what new messages they have received. This can be vital to people who need to be kept abreast of information and situations that may have occurred while they have been away from their desk.

E-mail is a cheap facility and costs just as much as the length of time it takes to send the message. It also cuts down the cost of paper memos and letters, and not all messages received have to be printed out, therefore reducing the stationery bill considerably.

There are many advantages and disadvantages with any communication system. E-mail has grown in popularity over the past few years, probably in accompaniment with access to the Internet, and will no doubt be around, in some form or other, for many years to come.

ELEMENT 3

ACCESS STORED INFORMATION SYSTEM

Performance criteria

(a) Specified stored information systems accessed and checked to be available.

(b) Customer queries are formatted correctly to meet requirements.

(c) Stored information system is correctly accessed in accordance with regulations.

(d) Information retrieved is verified to be timely, correct and meets customer requirements.

Range statement

(1) STORED INFORMATION SYSTEM Electronic mail, bulletin boards, databases, local, remote.

(2) QUERIES Structured, unstructured.

(3) REGULATIONS Organisation's legislation, equipment manufacturer's, software supplier's, health and safety, information provider.

Evidence required

Formatted queries used to access information system.

Details of requirements.

Observation of the candidate at work over a period of time accessing at least one local and one remote information system.

Evidence for this element may come from a realistic working environment.

Questioning is used where necessary to confirm specified knowledge.

We have looked at the transmission and receiving of information and messages utilising electronic media – fax, e-mail and bulletin boards. Now, we need to turn our attention to accessing stored information.

THE INTERNET

The main facility that falls into this category is that of the Internet. Originally it was conceived by the United States military as a way to protect its main computer facilities in the event of a nuclear war. This facility caught on, and very soon we had the birth of the Internet.

Since the early '90s, access and availability has grown for both business and personal use. It is basically a group of networks linked together – world-wide. The main pieces of equipment that are necessary for access to the Internet are: a computer, a modem, a telephone link or dedicated phone line, and subscription to a Service Provider.

Service Providers give access to the Internet via their bank of computers which have constant access to the Internet, and by tapping into them, you can access the Internet direct. Your computer uses the modem to contact their computers and in so doing, your computer becomes part of the chain as well. Most Service Providers charge a monthly fee, plus connection time. This is in addition to an initial joining fee *and* the calls that you are charged for on your phone bill. There are many Service Providers to choose from, so look carefully at what they offer and the charges that they make. Some will offer discount rates, no joining fee, or so many months free of charge, but read the small print before you join, as using the Internet can become a very expensive hobby, or even a way of life.

Once you have accessed a site on the Internet that you are interested in, you will able to view a number of pages which are connected using hyperlinks. These links provide the user with the ability to 'surf the net' and explore the millions of pages that are relevant to the topic in question. The pages contain text, graphics, photographs, sound and video-clips. It is all displayed effortlessly on your screen. HyperText Mark-up Language (HTML) is the language that the system uses to make many of the pages interlink and offer you the choice of information that is displayed before you.

Browsers also help the user to read and access the software used on the Internet, and to move or navigate around the pages. They will also help you to download any information that you want to keep, and print it out for you. Always ensure that you check for viruses after you have downloaded material from the Internet, as the risk of infection increases dramatically when 'surfing the net'. There are so many users and connections that the viruses can easily be transmitted from one system to another and may go undetected, if not regularly checked.

Access to a desired topic can be done in a number of ways. Type in the address, if you know it, so that the system moves directly to it; or, if you do not know the address, use the Search facility. Type in a word associated with the topic and use the search engine to seek out all the occurrences of the word. This is much more time-consuming and will also give you many instances of the word which may not be appropriate. Connections may also not be available using this facility, and it may be a case of trying again later, when connections are less busy, or trying to find a direct address to utilise more successfully.

Time and infinite patience are two of the main requirements for 'surfing the net'. It is often a very slow and laborious task, but you do have to remember that it is not just accessing computer systems around the corner, or even in the next county, or country, but WORLD-WIDE!

The Internet offers an e-mail facility and the ability to transmit messages globally. This can be particularly useful for business and organisations, and even on a personal level for those with specific interests and hobbies. Technology is forever developing and advancing. The Internet is part of the business world of today, and will increase its facilities and capabilities with incredible speed. Everyone wants to join in, so it is continuing to grow into the most enormous facility that we can imagine. World-wide communication is no longer a pipe dream: it is a reality through the utilisation of File Transfer Protocol (FTP), and the possibility of promoting, transmitting and receiving data world-wide is here to stay. No longer do we have to contain our business to the area we find ourselves based in. The internet is much more ambitious than that, and is developing both tools and techniques to make it bigger *and* better *and* faster in the foreseeable future.

The Internet does not have any controls imposed on it, nor does it have any restrictions. It provides open access to everyone and everything. Many problems have arisen as a result of this, and within the next year or so controls and restrictions will be implemented to safeguard the users. Access to the Internet is being encouraged in schools, and this is a good thing; but with no safeguards or restrictions, it is too easy to find things which we do not want children to have access to. Pornographic material and other material of an offensive nature can be easily located on the Internet for example.

Browse carefully and be cautious about information that may give you details about purchasing items, or asking you for your credit card details. Take care before you commit yourself to anything, as it may be particularly difficult to stop an item being despatched from the States, once you have pressed the button.

The Internet is a wealth of information, a giant library at your fingertips and often a joy and delight to use. It can also offer unique opportunities to obtain information for projects and homework assignments, the like of which has never been seen before. Make the most of the opportunity to explore and revel in the material at your fingertips, but remember that you can also find yourself in an expensive situation both through the cost of access, as well as through many of the shopping and spending facilities which will be available to you.

Practical Application:

How would you impose restrictions and controls on the Internet? Would it be a 'pay to play' facility or password protection, or even some other method? Do overall tighter controls need to be imposed on all information facilities, or just those of a 'hazardous ' nature? How would you impose this?

All our personal information is held on a variety of databases – list the ones you are likely to feature on, and describe how this was achieved. Do you want to be on them? Was it of your own choosing, or not? How would you go about curbing additional entry onto other databases?

> *Produce a detailed report to highlight the area and questions detailed above. Include personal experiences and ideals as you feel appropriate, and also include all relevant material in your portfolio of evidence.*

External databases

External databases exist mainly for references purposes. The Internet provides users with access to many of them, although often they have limited or restricted access as they may be a facility for subscribers only.

Airlines, travel agents and tour operators all need to have access to external databases for availability of flights and holidays. These systems are known as 'real time' systems. That means that if Brenda at Sure Flight books two seats on a flight from Glasgow to Paris, then when Sue at Travel Direct looks to see how many seats are left, there will be two less than there were when Brenda booked them for her customers. The system is constantly being updated to show the current situation.

Other organisations that use external databases include stock exchanges, for dealing in stocks and shares and, on a smaller scale, spare parts for cars. These can be located using the database to ascertain stock levels and availability. Some offer the user the opportunity to interact with the information that the system is showing – like the travel agents, booking the seats on the flight. Others just exist to give you the information that you require, and the additional facilities that may be available are just for the subscribers.

Think of some external databases which you may know about or use. What are they for? How do you use them? Are they interactive, or just for information only? Can anyone access them, or do you have to pay to view? Write a brief description of the facility that you use, and its advantages and disadvantages.

CONCLUSION

COMMUNICATE ELECTRONICALLY USING INFORMATION TECHNOLOGY SOLUTION

Completion of this Unit will demonstrate that you can:
- Utilise electronic communication media for both the transmission and receipt of messages and information;
- Utilise stored information either through a database, or the Internet;
- Communicate effectively with both people and electronic equipment;
- Name a number of different communication facilities;
- Maintain confidentiality at all times;
- Print out messages from the medium used;
- Understand and maximise the potential of any equipment utilised within the organisation as an essential part of today's technology and an integral aspect of the electronic office.

CONGRATULATIONS – YOU HAVE NOW SUCCESSFULLY COMPLETED UNIT EIGHT!

To tie up all the loose ends covered in this Unit, try to complete the Unit 8 exercise to produce additional evidence for inclusion in your portfolio.

EXERCISE

This exercise takes the guise of a minor project, and consists of a comprehensive investigation into the background, capabilities, and possible costs of implementing a suitable system and facilities for the use of e-mail, facsimile, bulletin boards and the Internet, within an organisation.

Research into each element is essential. Similarly, you should provide supporting evidence of the service providers, installation and equipment necessary to facilitate such a system, as well as additional and on-going expenditure to enable continuous use after it has been installed. There are many books and journals available on the market which will help with this aspect. You could also utilise the Internet itself, if you already have access to it, to explore and discover the best facilities and providers available, as well as to find a wealth of information on the subject which will be an asset within the format of this project.

With regard to the facsimile, it does have to be an integral system: one that can be used within the structure of a computer and not a stand-alone facility, so as to become part of a totally electronic communication system.

It would perhaps be a good idea to produce a User's Guide on getting started, and to include all your material and information in here, under suitable sections and/or headings. Tips and explanations could also be included, so that a comprehensive booklet is produced that can be used in conjunction with the implemented system, or when the user needs additional information to help them use the system to its maximum potential.

There is much to investigate and research, and hopefully it will whet your appetite for the taste of things to come in the technological future.

VIDEO BONANZA

	PRICE PER DAY	DAYS' HIRE	TOTAL COST (B4*C4)	EXTENDED HIRE SPECIAL OFFER PRICE	SAVING	PRICE PER DAY INCREASE OF 10%	SPECIAL OFFER PRICE INCREASE OF 5%
TELETUBBIES	£1.50	66	£99.00	£5.00		£1.65	£5.25
PRETTY WOMAN	£1.00	19	£19.00	£2.50		£1.10	£2.63
ALIEN	£1.00	14	£14.00	£2.50		£1.10	£2.63
DELIA SMITH'S COOKERY CLASS	£1.00	12	£12.00	£2.50		£1.10	£2.63
TWINS	£1.00	12	£12.00	£2.50		£1.10	£2.63
SCRUPLES	£1.00	12	£12.00	£2.50		£1.10	£2.63
AINSLEY'S BARBECUES	£1.00	11	£11.00	£2.50		£1.10	£2.63
DUMBO	£0.50	5	£2.50	£1.00		£0.55	£1.05
STAR TREK - THE FINAL FRONTIER	£1.00	4	£4.00	£2.50		£1.10	£2.63
TOP GUN	£1.00	3	£3.00	£2.50	£0.50	£1.10	£2.63
LETHAL WEAPON	£1.00	3	£3.00	£2.50	£0.50	£1.10	£2.63
CAN'T COOK WON'T COOK	£1.00	3	£3.00	£2.50	£0.50	£1.10	£2.63
STAR WARS - TRILOGY	£1.00	3	£3.00	£2.50	£0.50	£1.10	£2.63
K9	£1.00	3	£3.00	£2.50	£0.50	£1.10	£2.63
BARNEY AND FRIENDS	£0.50	3	£1.50	£1.00	£0.50	£0.55	£1.05
WINNIE THE POOH AND FRIENDS	£0.50	3	£1.50	£1.00	£0.50	£0.55	£1.05
LIVE AND LET DIE	£1.00	2	£2.00	£2.50		£1.10	£2.63
GOLDFINGER	£1.00	2	£2.00	£2.50		£1.10	£2.63
TURNER AND HOOCH	£1.00	2	£2.00	£2.50		£1.10	£2.63
BEETHOVEN	£1.00	1	£1.00	£2.50		£1.10	£2.63

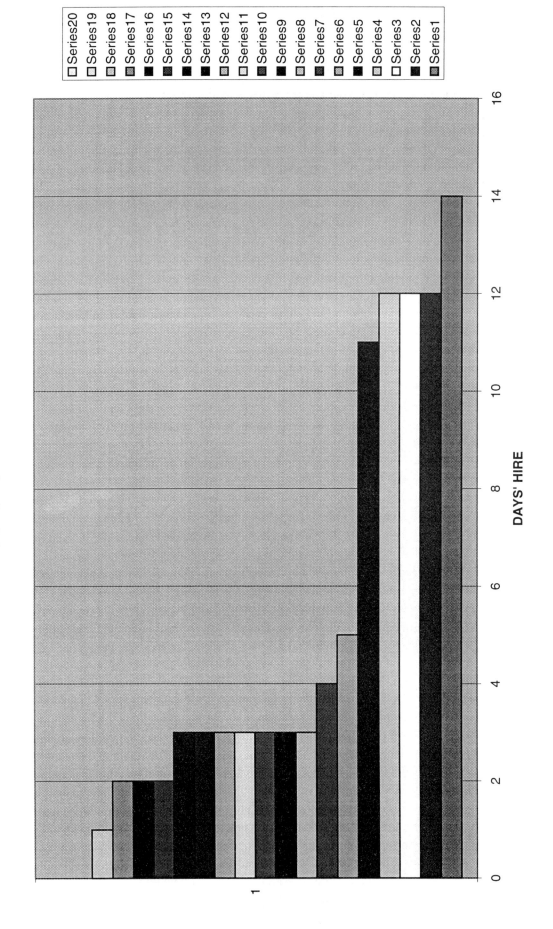

GRAPH OF TITLES BY POPULARITY

TITLES 1 - 20

DAYS' HIRE

VIDEO BONANZA

Good news everyone, videos are now **EXTRA CHEAP** to rent, which is especially good news as the Easter Holidays are nearly with us again, and it is never easy to keep the children amused when the weather is uncertain!

Well here's the answer!

Rent a selection of videos to keep them entertained at special offer prices, and they will be happy for hours. Over the page is a graph which highlights our top twenty titles – there are plenty of others to choose from too.   SEE YOU SOON.

VIDEO BONANZA

TITLES 1 - 20

Series	Title
Series20	BEETHOVEN
Series19	LIVE AND LET DIE
Series18	GOLDFINGER
Series17	TURNER AND HOOCH
Series16	TOP GUN
Series15	LETHAL WEAPON
Series14	CAN'T COOK WON'T COOK
Series13	STAR WARS - TRILOGY
Series12	K9
Series11	BARNEY AND FRIENDS
Series10	WINNIE THE POOH AND FRIENDS
Series9	STAR TREK - THE FINAL FRONTIER
Series8	DUMBO
Series7	AINSLEY'S BARBECUES
Series6	DELIA SMITH'S COCKERY CLASS
Series5	TWINS
Series4	SCRUPLES
Series3	ALIEN
Series2	PRETTY WOMAN
Series1	TELETUBBIES

DAYS' HIRE

UNIT 7

ELEMENT 1

Enter data to create and update images

Performance criteria

(a) Authority to access files and images is obtained as necessary.

(b) Sources of files and images required are correctly identified and located.

(c) Images are entered completely using appropriate input device correctly and to schedule.

(d) Files saved conform to organisation's agreed standards.

Range statement

(1) FILE New, existing.

(2) IMAGES Bitmap, vector.

(3) INPUT DEVICE Keyboard, selection device, scanner.

(4) ORGANISATION'S STANDARDS Naming convention, location, frequency.

Evidence required

Vector and bitmap images entered by the candidate.

Observation of the candidate at work over a period of time entering images.

Evidence for this element may come from a realistic working environment.

Questioning is used where necessary to confirm specified knowledge.

The information detailed here covers all the elements necessary for you to successfully complete and attain Unit 7. Some questions or exercises are indicated as we go along and are typed in *italics*.

Try to make notes about each subject covered as you come across it within your college or work placement tasks, so that at the end of the Unit, completion of the Competence Statement will not be so time-consuming or difficult. It is often a good idea to have extra copies of the blank forms to hand so that you can jot down the elements you cover as you go, and then just rewrite/type your notes for a comprehensive and well documented statement.

Enter data to create and update images

Like most of the files/documents we have been dealing with, you always need to obtain the appropriate authority before you utilise an existing file, if it is not your own. Check the filename and make sure that you select the correct one, once authority has been granted.

Tasks are often given as a completely new job, and if so, this is a case of starting from scratch. When this occurs, make sure that you completely understand all the requirements, and that you feel confident to complete the task within the given timescale. If there appears to be a problem, sort it out sooner rather than later. Seek the advice and assist-ance of the customer concerned, or speak to your supervisor for his input on the subject.

Some existing files are stored in different locations, and often these are accessed through a variety of levels of passwords. These levels protect the data and information that is stored there. If you are given the authority to access them direct, and are trusted with the appropriate passwords, do not write them down, or divulge them to anyone else. The maintenance and security of the data and the integrity of the system is vital at all times, and it is easy to neglect the safety of the data by leaving the passwords around for others to see and use.

Once you are totally sure of the requirements, and exactly what you have to produce and by when, you can proceed to load up an appropriate software package for the task in hand.

What software can and do you use, and why?

If you do not have a full-blown desktop publishing or graphics package available to use, you can still produce a wide variety of documents and graphics by using the clip art facility in many word-processing packages.

To be able to use the facilities to their best advantage, a number of input devices are available to use. The most popular are the keyboard and mouse, but nowadays scanners are used extensively to input images, photographs and text into computer format. Lightpens and trackballs are also used, but have more specific uses than the keyboard and mouse. Lightpens offer greater control when dealing with complex and technical images, and trackballs are usually found on laptop computers.

What sort of input device do you use, and why? Do you have access to a scanner? If so, scan in a photograph, a graphic image and a piece of text. Produce three separate documents for inclusion in your portfolio of evidence. If you do not have access to a scanner, find out about the different types of scanners available, cost and capabilities.

Save any work that you produce to the correct location and using the appropriate naming convention. Print out any documents you have produced, and make sure that they do not contain confidential or sensitive material. If they do, write about how you created and produced them, and perhaps illustrate this information with copies of the graphic you used, omitting the sensitive areas, thus demonstrating your ability to utilise graphics confidently and competently.

Unit 7

There are two main sorts of graphic image, and these are VECTOR GRAPHICS and BITMAP IMAGES.

Vector graphics are made up of lines and will be used mainly to construct precise and complex images, technical drawings and other images created by, for example, the drawing office. They are often constructed using specialist packages and high powered and very expensive computer-aided-design (CAD) equipment. CAD systems also offer a rotational aspect or view on screen, so that the user can see all around the image. This can also be thought of as a 3D (three-dimensional) image. Computer games use this type of vector graphic image for the graphics that they contain. As many of you will no doubt know, the quality of computer games has developed drastically over the past ten or twelve years: they are far superior and more complex than they were originally.

Bitmap images basically consist of blocks or colour, and the majority of packages use this form today. Clip art and graphic images, contained in software, are effectively used to produce professional documents and to enhance their general production: these too are bitmap images.

Bitmap images can be reshaped, resized and recoloured according to your personal requirements. You should always remember to take care when reshaping or resizing, as it is easy to distort the image, and it will not look as good as it did before you started altering it.

There are many graphics packages available to help you to produce excellent graphics, as well as a vast number of desktop publishing and presentation products. Look at your requirement before investing in any software, and ascertain if it will give you the freedom you need, and also that it will accomplish 99% of the tasks that you are required to undertake.

Copyright is an another aspect that needs to be considered here. Always read the small print on any licensing agreement, and also reread Unit 5.3 for further detailed information on the subject.

ELEMENT 2

Produce required graphical image by manipulating data

Performance criteria

(a) Customer graphical image requirements are accurately established, verified and checked.

(b) Options for graphical image are identified, and preferred solution agreed with customer.

(c) Facilities to enter, select and combine stored images are correctly used to meet requirements.

(d) Facilities are selected and used correctly to manipulate image.

(e) Facilities to create additional elements are used correctly to meet requirements.

(f) Facilities to alter attributes are used correctly to meet requirements.

(g) Graphical image is checked to be complete and to meet customer requirements.

Range statement

(1) FACILITIES Size, location, orientation, rotation, invert.

(2) ATTRIBUTES Colour, shade, patterns, size, shape.

(3) ADDITIONAL ELEMENTS Line, shape, text.

Evidence required

Three graphical images produced, covering the range.

Details of customer requirements.

Observation of the candidate at work over a period of time establishing customer requirements for a graphical image.

Evidence for this element may come from a realistic working environment.

Questioning is used where necessary to confirm specified knowledge.

Manipulating data, as we have discussed before, gives you the ability to update an existing file. Choose one that will be appropriate for this element and make sure that it doesn't matter if you change its format. If you have been given a specific task for this element, then so much the better; if not, design a suitable document for yourself.

Unit 7

Practical Application and UNIT 7 - EXERCISE:

Select your document, either in agreement with your customer or supervisor, or through your own choice, as a suitable file for this exercise.

Firstly, print out a copy of the document, if it is an existing one, so that you have a 'before and after' image to refer to.

Next, change the page orientation from landscape to portrait, or vice versa. Decrease or increase the margins around all the sides so that the overall size changes. Select one of the graphics contained within its structure – it should now appear with black handles on all the way round, and reshape and resize it, by dragging on any one of these handles. This will now have totally changed both the page orientation, layout and graphic on the page.

Returning to the graphic, select it again and move its position on the page. Next, change its colour. Add other suitable graphics to complement the context of the document and print out the whole document in its revised format.

If you do not have a suitable existing document to use for this exercise, create one using the following:

Open a new document in either a word-processing package or graphics application, and with the page in portrait layout, design a page which will include both text and graphics. A poster is an ideal choice as this gives you ample opportunity to combine the two requirements on the one page, and in an interesting format.

Input appropriate text in a suitable font; change the size and typeface accordingly. Choose colours if you have a colour printer; if not, patterns or shading to make the images bold and eye-catching. Resize it as required and add further text or images to fill the page. The combination of text and images works well.

Check for any obvious errors and then print out your finished poster. Combine this with a detailed explanation of how you achieved it, and include it in your portfolio of evidence. Also include any additional material or information that was given to you as part of a predetermined task. Highlight, in the explanation, any areas of difficulty, and also those aspects which you manipulated, changed, created and also combined together to achieve the end result.

Unit 7

ELEMENT 3

Output specified image to destination

Performance criteria

(a) Appropriate destination is correctly selected.

(b) The destination device is checked to ensure that it is able to receive output.

(c) Image is verified to be complete and correct prior to output.

(d) Output parameters are identified and set up correctly to meet customer requirements.

(e) Image is sent to correct destination.

(f) Output is checked to be complete and meets the customer's requirements.

Range statement

(1) DESTINATION Local, remote.

(2) DESTINATION DEVICE Hard copy, magnetic storage.

(3) OUTPUT PARAMETERS Page range, number of copies, colour.

Evidence required

Output of three graphical images, covering the range.

Details of customer requirements.

Observation of the candidate at work over a period of time producing required output.

Evidence for this element may come from a realistic working environment.

Questioning is used where necessary to confirm specified knowledge.

(This information is much the same as for Unit 6.4, as both these units deal with sending specific images to a printer, or destination.)

Printing your graphic image or document after you have checked all the data is the final stage. If you are fortunate enough to have a colour printer, then so much the better as the colours will add an extra dimension to the graphical representation.

Before you set the printer running, there are a few checks that you need to undertake so that you do not waste paper and the end result is of a high standard.

First, make sure that the printer is switched on and that it is ready to receive your data – this is called being ON LINE. Another thing to check is the ink/toner – make sure there is sufficient for your whole print run. If you have to find someone to change the cartridge or replace the toner, you will need to restart your print from the required page.

Output specified image to destination

What sort of ink/toner does your printer use? Can you change the cartridge yourself, or do you have to get a technician/supervisor to do it for you?

Paper is another factor worth checking. Make sure there is plenty available, and that it is the type that you require. Graphics are usually printed on plain paper and not headed paper, unless for a special reason. Check the printer trays and send the print via the plain paper tray, or refill the upper or single tray with plain paper. Don't overfill it, or the printer will jam.

What sort of paper does your printer use? Which tray does it use, if there is more than one available?

If your printer experiences a problem, try and sort it out, or get someone who can. Never try and clear the problem by switching it off and on again. We are all tempted to do this, but it can and does cause bigger problems later on. It can also lose work that is already in the buffer and waiting to be printed.

What do you do when your printer develops a fault? Detail the procedure you follow and why it is important to do so.

Planning and forethought will help to eliminate many problems associated with printing and the output of your documents.

We discussed the use of T-switches in Unit 2.3. Reread this to confirm what you may need to know about how to utilise them successfully. Manuals and User Guides are also vital books to have to hand as they will often guide you through some of the problems that you may incur, and also how to use the machine correctly. Treat them with respect, as they are a delicate piece of hardware and can easily go wrong. They need regular servicing and maintenance to prolong their life. With this, and the use of the correct ink/toner and appropriate paper, it will work reliably for you for many hours at a time. Always check the paper type first, as many printers will not produce quality output if substandard paper is used. Look after them, and they will run trouble free for many years and produce reliable and professional documents for you.

Sometimes large and complex graphic images are printed remotely, rather than tying up a small local printer for ages, or they can even be plotted. Plotting gives a much finer and more accurate final image, and is used extensively for large technical drawings, and other computer-aided-design drawings and images. It also offers the possibility of printing on a much larger scale, which is often beneficial for scaled-up and down drawings. Sizes range from A0 to A1.

Find out all about plotters, costs and capabilities. Does your organisation have a plotter? If so, what does it print and why?

Always save your work regularly and to the correct location, using the appropriate naming convention. If you are printing remotely, make sure that the connection between computer and printer/plotter is in place, otherwise save the file to a suitable floppy disk or network facility which you will be able to access from another computer. By saving the file to disk, you are then able to utilise it nearer the location of the plotter, or other suitable printer. Floppy disks are portable, and providing that the other computer has the appropriate software loaded, access is quick and easy. Similarly, if you save it to a net-work facility, access it again at the computer linked into the plotter, and away you go. Always check first that you are not jumping a queue, as often these large printers and plotters get very busy with long-winded jobs, so be prepared to wait. I assure you that the end result will be stunning!

Unit 7

CONCLUSION

Produce graphical images using information technology solution

Completion of this Unit will demonstrate that you can:

- Access suitable software for producing graphics and images;
- Understand appropriate copyright legislation;
- Create and update graphic images using a variety of different software packages and facilities;
- Rotate, resize, reshape, recolour, invert and add suitable attributes to an existing or created image or graphic;
- Sort out any problems associated with using graphics;
- Print the final version to a printer or plotter;
- Save the files to floppy disk or network facility for printing locally or remotely.

CONGRATULATIONS – YOU HAVE NOW SUCCESSFULLY COMPLETED UNIT SEVEN!

To tie up all the loose ends covered in this Unit, try to complete the Unit 7 exercise to produce additional evidence for inclusion in your portfolio.

UNIT 8

ELEMENT 1

Transmit messages using information technology

Performance criteria

(a) Appropriate facilities for transmitting messages are selected.

(b) Messages to be transmitted are checked for completeness and accuracy prior to transmission.

(c) Appropriate transmission parameters are correctly entered.

(d) Messages are transmitted correctly, completely and to regulations.

Range statement

(1) FACILITIES Electronic mail, bulletin boards, facsimile.

(2) TRANSMISSION PARAMETERS Name, reference address, number of copies.

(3) REGULATIONS Organisation's, legislation, equipment manufacturer's, software supplier's, health and safety.

Evidence required

Observation of the candidate at work over a period of time using two different transmission facilities.

Evidence for this element may come from a realistic working environment.

Questioning is used where necessary to confirm specified knowledge.

The information detailed here covers all the elements necessary for you to successfully complete and attain Unit 8. Some questions or exercises are indicated as we go along and are typed in *italics*.

Try to make notes about each subject covered as you come across it within your college or work placement tasks, so that at the end of the Unit, completion of the Competence Statement will not be so time consuming or difficult. It is often a good idea to have extra copies of the blank forms to hand so that you can jot down the elements you cover as you go, and then just rewrite/type your notes for a comprehensive and well documented statement.

Transmit messages using information technology

Today, communication is an essential aspect of our working lives, and it takes a variety of forms. We can communicate verbally – face to face, or over the phone. We can send each other memos, letters, reports and other documents through the internal or external mail system. Similarly, we can send written information by electronic means by using a facsimile (fax) machine, or a computer and e-mail.

This element looks at transmitting messages, i.e. *sending* them to others. We can use either a fax or e-mail facility for this.

Facsimile Machines (FAX)

Fax machines are mostly thought of as stand-alone machines, and for the purpose of this element we need to disregard these because, although they are a means of communication, they do not fall into the electronic communication aspect that we are to consider here.

When you send a fax, it is instant. All you need is the address of the recipient: key this in, press SEND and away it goes! Most organisations have fax machines, so it is likely that you will be able to send documents and information to almost all of them. Directories containing fax numbers are also published, so looking up a number is relatively easy. Costs are comparatively low, and you do know that the information goes directly there, and will not get lost in the post.

Many fax machines use ordinary photocopy paper, so again the cost is at a minimum. Do, however, take care not to overload them as they easily jam up and then no one will be able to get through.

Integral faxes offer exactly the same facilities as stand-alone ones, but they are part of your computer, thus keeping extra equipment to a minimum. This is ideal for a small workstation, or office. It does, however, mean that you have to have a dedicated phone line to facilitate the link, but this is most commonly utilised for access to the Internet and e-mail as well, so it has a multi-function and will justify initial expenditure.

Whatever type of fax machine you have, you will need to make sure that you can operate it correctly. Always include a front cover with your document, so that the receiver knows who it is for, how many pages it contains in total, and who to contact if it comes through illegibly, as is sometimes the case.

> *What sort of fax do you use? Does it use ordinary cut A4 paper, or special fax rolls? Do you use a standard front sheet, or just make up one when you need to? Include a copy of your front sheet, as well as a fax that you have transmitted to someone. Highlight the address/number it is going to, your name and number, as well as the number of pages sent. You may also get a transmission report after you have successfully sent a fax: include this as well. If you do not have a standard front sheet to use, design a suitable one and include it here as well.*
>
> *Also, obtain some information about other types of fax machine, especially if the one you use is a stand-alone. Obtain the necessary details about an integral one. Costs, capabilities and facilities are also useful here.*

The cost of sending a fax is incurred by the length of time that it takes to send the information down the telephone line. The quicker it goes, the cheaper it is. Graphics take longer to send, so the price increases. Similarly, a page full of text, with very little 'white space', will take longer to send.

Faxes, like e-mail, come into their own when there is a postal strike, as they enable communication to continue electronically regardless of the external facilities that are available.

Transmission reports are produced after each transmission sent, or if preferred, these can be produced after a quantity of faxes have been sent. They offer the sender the opportunity to check the fax number used, yet again, and to see whether or not the fax was sent at the first time of trying, or if it had to wait until the line was free, and if so, if it was transmitted in full, or if there was a problem with transmission. Error numbers may be recorded on this report for the sender to pick up on and understand fully the nature of the problem that occurred. It is often easier to write the number '3' instead of:

> **The line was busy, so tried again later, but then I couldn't transmit in full as their machine ran out of paper!!!**

Electronic Mail (e-mail)

This is a method of electronic communication between computers that are linked together. They can be linked by a LAN – local area network. A LAN is a link that runs between departments, rooms, offices, buildings or sites next to each other. For links further afield, you have to utilise either telephone lines or a WAN – wide area network. Some e-mail packages that are connected to a WAN will be able to link up globally. This is especially useful for communication between colleagues for business or pleasure, or for the more serious facility of conducting business quickly and easily. It is possible to pass orders onto suppliers from customers, and vice versa – this is all possible through the use of Electronic Data Interchange (EDI).

To use e-mail, you need to have an address or mail box: what it is called depends on the type of system in use. An address is just like your postal address. Friends and relatives need to know it to send you letters, just as the postman needs to know it to deliver your letters. When other users know your e-mail address, they can send you mail electronically.

With most e-mail facilities it is possible to send documents and attachments along with your message. This is great for important documents that you want to get to someone prior to a meeting, and it may take a while in the post!

Most e-mail systems are quick and easy to use, and in many organisations it has taken over from traditional paper memos and letters. It has been known to improve all levels of communication, and even more so when it is implemented with a training session, so that the users get to understand, first-hand, its capabilities and how to use it efficiently.

One of the first things to learn is to re-read your message before you send it, as it is often too late to recall it once you have pressed the SEND button, and you can look foolish if there are errors in the text, or worse still if you send it to the wrong person by mistyping the address

Transmit messages using information technology

One of the main advantages of using e-mail is that you can read the information as soon as you receive it, which often is instantaneous. Timing may depend on the distance that the message is travelling. You can add notes onto the end of a received e-mail and send the whole lot back again to the sender – all at the touch of a button. However, although your message is transmitted and received in an instant, there is no guarantee that the receiver will actually read it there and then. They may be in a meeting, on holiday or off sick, and will not be able to read their new mail until they return to their desk.

There are many shortcuts to using some e-mail systems, and as you become a more experienced user, you will become aware of these.

Do you use e-mail? If so, what is it called? How often do you read your messages? How do you know if you have any? Can you print out your messages direct from the screen or via a word-processing package?

Investigate the concept of transmitting messages via e-mail, and write a brief report on its associated advantages and disadvantages.

Sending messages via e-mail to a number of people is also simple. It may be that you have compiled lists of people who perhaps go to the same meetings and therefore need to have copies of the documents sent to them in advance, or people who work in the same department. You can, of course, also distribute to everyone at the same time; this usually comes under the heading of ALL, and is used for general and informal broadcasts or a personal message, but make sure you really want it to go to everyone first!

'DRINKS ARE ON ME AT LUNCHTIME – SEE YOU AT THE PUB!'

Always read all your messages: they may contain useful, important or even urgent information. Also check and make sure that all the information is readable. Typing mistakes can often detract or confuse a vital point, or even distort the whole context of the message.

Regular users of e-mail have developed their own language and abbreviations to speed up their keying-in. There is also a code of conduct which they abide by; it is also utilised on the Bulletin Board facility that we shall be looking at shortly.

This code of practice is called 'NETIQUETTE'. Basically, it suggests that you do not type in capital letters as this gives the impression of shouting. If you want to *emphasise* a word, place it between asterisks, and so on.

Find out more about NETIQUETTE.

The process of speeding up the keying-in takes place through the use of acronyms, or three letter acronyms – TLAs, and some examples of these are:

        BTW – by the way

        FYI – for your information

        KISS – keep it simple, stupid

There are many others which are used regularly, find some out for yourselves.

Another way that has developed to show feeling electronically is through the use of 'emoticons'. These are usually in the format of shapes and symbols which are placed in the written text to show how a user is feeling, or to add depth of feeling to the message.

:-) or :) fun or amusement

:-(or :(sad or disappointed

;-) winking – believe it if you will!

The general term which refers to these graphic displays within the written text is 'smileys.' :-)

Never use the e-mail facility to send angry messages, especially if using the e-mail or Bulletin Board facilities on the Internet. Angry messages are referred to as a 'flame', and if sent to a group of people, can result in 'flame war', so be careful what you write, and more so HOW you write it. Check and double check the contents of your message. Think of the tone in which it is written, and how it will be received. Also, give some thought to your heading or title, as many users who receive mountains of mail may skip boring-looking messages and read only what they feel is interesting by the sound of the title.

PAUL AND MARY TAKE THE PLUNGE

or

BIRTHS, DEATHS AND MARRIAGES

To end your e-mail message, you need to add a 'signature'. This is a piece of text which you add onto the end of your messages, and which contains information about you, the sender. It may contain your name, company name, phone number, e-mail address, and any other information which may be essential. Most 'signatures' should be between four and seven lines long: any longer and it can take over the message!

Bulletin Board Services (BBS)

This facility is similar to e-mail, but it is usually linked to a Service Provider as an additional facility for their subscribers, or a large organisation which has implemented this facility for themselves. Bulletin Boards or BBSs allow users to exchange information and interact with each other. Some e-mail systems give you the option to interact, but BBSs tend to have the monopoly over them for this facility.

BBSs also have the upper hand when it comes to linking and communication on a global scale. Large international organisations which work around the globe may utilise this facility extensively, especially if there is a major project underway. It may be that one part is being manufactured in the States, another in Germany, and it is all being assembled in the UK. Communication is vital, and much time is spent by personnel commuting between countries, if they are not holding videoconferences.

Minutes of meetings need to be sent to *all* interested parties in the project, and one way to do this is to post them onto a BBS. Everyone involved with the project will know of its existence and location, plus any passwords which may be necessary to protect the information stored there. Once the meeting has been held, the minutes are typed up and posted onto the BBS. When the personnel arrive for work at each associated site, internationally, they access the BBS, and find there the information they need from the last meeting. The BBS allows them the opportunity to add notes and amendments to the text, usually in italics, capital letters, or a different font, so as to differentiate who it is from, and it is returned to the sender, updated. This is much quicker than sending the minutes by fax, as nothing can be added to this without retyping it; or by post, as it can take several days for mail to get around the world.

You need to check your BBS regularly to see if any additional information has been received or updated. It is not an efficient facility if you do not do this.

Most BBS facilities are simple to use, although there is always some element of risk when posting information to a facility such as this. Make sure that it is well password-protected, and that only users who need to use the facility know of its whereabouts and existence. That way, you can minimise the risk as much as possible.

Delete old files, and only keep what is current on the system otherwise it will become overloaded, but always take a copy of the transmissions for future reference because once a file has been deleted, it cannot be retrieved.

Copies of appropriate data taken from the BBS can be easily copied again and distributed to interested parties, and careful and continued use of the system will offer realistic and efficient facilities to those who use it.

BBSs that Service Providers offer, facilitate the same type of capabilities, but for subscribers only, as a general notice board for those with a common interest or hobby: a place where they can exchange views, ideals and ideas, and a rare opportunity to interact with each other on a world-wide scale.

Electronic technology has grown enormously over the last decade, especially where transmission and communication are concerned. It is now faster and works globally as well. As the old proverb says:

"The world's my oyster"

I wonder what they would have said if they had known what we know today!

Unit 8

ELEMENT 2

RECEIVE MESSAGES USING INFORMATION TECHNOLOGY

Performance criteria

(a) Appropriate facilities for receiving messages are correctly selected and made ready.

(b) Appropriate location is regularly checked for messages.

(c) Messages received are checked for completeness and accuracy.

(d) Messages received in error are referred to appropriate authority.

(e) Messages are correctly processed to regulations.

Range statement

(1) FACILITIES Electronic mail, bulletin boards, facsimile.

(2) MESSAGES Structured, unstructured.

(3) APPROPRIATE AUTHORITY Sender, line manager, supervisor.

(4) REGULATIONS Organisation's, legislation, equipment manufacturer's, software supplier's, health and safety.

Evidence required

Two messages received using two different facilities.

Observation of the candidate at work over a period of time using receiving equipment.

Evidence for this element may come from a realistic working environment.

Questioning is used where necessary to confirm specified knowledge.

Receiving messages electronically, using either fax or e-mail, means that you have to have your system constantly ready to receive any input. The printer connected to the system also needs to have a constant supply of paper, so that it too can print out any fax messages that it receives. Depending upon how the computer has been configured and set up, it does not have to be switched on for it to receive incoming messages. With e-mail, it will receive them automatically and log them in your mailbox ready for you to read when you next start up your computer.

BBSs are slightly different: they are a facility provided as an additional service to subscribers, and normally to receive messages via this medium your computer has to be switched on.

Always check your system regularly for messages. Some systems play music when a new message is received, others have an icon of an envelope which opens to reveal a slip of paper. This signifies that a new message has been received.

Receive messages using information technology

What happens when you get a new message? If nothing happens to prompt you that you may have a new message, get into the habit of checking your mailbox, at least twice a day. Do you use your e-mail facility regularly? If so, what do you use it for? What are the advantages and disadvantages of this? Some messages often contain confidential material: be aware of this, and know how to deal with them appropriately, using company procedures.

Some e-mail packages often show you which messages you have read, and which are new ones, by a * star, or other symbol next to them, or they may appear as bold on the screen, or highlighted in some other way, so that the user can easily differentiate between old and new mail.

Most mail box facilities have a maximum capacity of messages that they can hold. You need to make sure that you delete any old or unimportant messages on a regular basis so that you always have plenty of room to receive new messages. If you keep too much in your mailbox, new messages won't be able to get through to you, and you may miss out on some important messages.

BBSs usually store all their information in a central location which all users or subscribers know about, so that they can readily access the information they need. A simple screen message may be sent to all interested parties to show them that new information has been received on the BBS, so that they know to access it at their earliest convenience. Again, much depends on the type of system and the facilities it utilises as to the way you receive your messages.

Some messages that are received follow a structured approach – in a direct response to a personal message they themselves received. Others may be more unstructured and available for everyone to read with no specific recipient named. The unstructured approach is the most common one utilised on BBSs – it is more of a general information service, whereas e-mail is named and specific, although of course messages can be sent and received by anyone (see 8.1 for more details on this).

Messages can be received in error – the wrong address used, or a simple typing error. If it looks important when you read it, but it has nothing to do with you, seek advice from your supervisor, or contact the sender direct for assistance on what they want you to do. Whatever action you take, always follow company procedures – it is better to be safe than sorry!

Messages that you receive may be sent to you so that you can forward printed information onto others who do not have an e-mail facility themselves. Print out the message you have received on their behalf, and forward it to the appropriate person as requested.

Paper copies of messages received are a good way of keeping track of important messages, and will help not to clutter up the system unnecessarily. Keep your mailbox accessible because when it is full you will be unable to receive new messages. Often, it is useful to be able to keep track of important information that you have received and also it may be necessary to substantiate any actions that you took as a result of a message received. If you delete the message from your mail box, then there is no trace or evidence left to substantiate your actions, but if you have paper proof, then it will be readily available, and may just get you out of deep water!

Unit 8

The main disadvantage of an e-mail facility is that you cannot sign any documents that you send, so the receiver has no proof of authentication. Anyone could have sent it! We looked at signatures in 8.1, but it is quite easy to replicate another person's if you have half a mind to. Some users have a special symbol that they use to authenticate what they send, so that the recipient knows that it is genuine.

How do you know if what you receive on e-mail is genuine or not? What would you like to see done to assist with this problem? What other disadvantages are there with the system that you use? Produce a document to highlight these, plus any other information that you feel would be of value to other users, and in particular recipients of e-mail, via a similar system.

On the other hand, e-mail is a very flexible service, and is especially useful for people who travel around, as it is possible for them to access their mailbox using a laptop or other computer system. They type in their access code and can then look into their mailbox and see what new messages they have received. This can be vital to people who need to be kept abreast of information and situations that may have occurred while they have been away from their desk.

E-mail is a cheap facility and costs just as much as the length of time it takes to send the message. It also cuts down the cost of paper memos and letters, and not all messages received have to be printed out, therefore reducing the stationery bill considerably.

There are many advantages and disadvantages with any communication system. E-mail has grown in popularity over the past few years, probably in accompaniment with access to the Internet, and will no doubt be around, in some form or other, for many years to come.

ELEMENT 3

ACCESS STORED INFORMATION SYSTEM

Performance criteria

(a) Specified stored information systems accessed and checked to be available.

(b) Customer queries are formatted correctly to meet requirements.

(c) Stored information system is correctly accessed in accordance with regulations.

(d) Information retrieved is verified to be timely, correct and meets customer requirements.

Range statement

(1) STORED INFORMATION SYSTEM Electronic mail, bulletin boards, databases, local, remote.

(2) QUERIES Structured, unstructured.

(3) REGULATIONS Organisation's legislation, equipment manufacturer's, software supplier's, health and safety, information provider.

Evidence required

Formatted queries used to access information system.

Details of requirements.

Observation of the candidate at work over a period of time accessing at least one local and one remote information system.

Evidence for this element may come from a realistic working environment.

Questioning is used where necessary to confirm specified knowledge.

We have looked at the transmission and receiving of information and messages utilising electronic media – fax, e-mail and bulletin boards. Now, we need to turn our attention to accessing stored information.

THE INTERNET

The main facility that falls into this category is that of the Internet. Originally it was conceived by the United States military as a way to protect its main computer facilities in the event of a nuclear war. This facility caught on, and very soon we had the birth of the Internet.

Since the early '90s, access and availability has grown for both business and personal use. It is basically a group of networks linked together – world-wide. The main pieces of equipment that are necessary for access to the Internet are: a computer, a modem, a telephone link or dedicated phone line, and subscription to a Service Provider.

Service Providers give access to the Internet via their bank of computers which have constant access to the Internet, and by tapping into them, you can access the Internet direct. Your computer uses the modem to contact their computers and in so doing, your computer becomes part of the chain as well. Most Service Providers charge a monthly fee, plus connection time. This is in addition to an initial joining fee *and* the calls that you are charged for on your phone bill. There are many Service Providers to choose from, so look carefully at what they offer and the charges that they make. Some will offer discount rates, no joining fee, or so many months free of charge, but read the small print before you join, as using the Internet can become a very expensive hobby, or even a way of life.

Once you have accessed a site on the Internet that you are interested in, you will able to view a number of pages which are connected using hyperlinks. These links provide the user with the ability to 'surf the net' and explore the millions of pages that are relevant to the topic in question. The pages contain text, graphics, photographs, sound and video-clips. It is all displayed effortlessly on your screen. HyperText Mark-up Language (HTML) is the language that the system uses to make many of the pages interlink and offer you the choice of information that is displayed before you.

Browsers also help the user to read and access the software used on the Internet, and to move or navigate around the pages. They will also help you to download any information that you want to keep, and print it out for you. Always ensure that you check for viruses after you have downloaded material from the Internet, as the risk of infection increases dramatically when 'surfing the net'. There are so many users and connections that the viruses can easily be transmitted from one system to another and may go undetected, if not regularly checked.

Access to a desired topic can be done in a number of ways. Type in the address, if you know it, so that the system moves directly to it; or, if you do not know the address, use the Search facility. Type in a word associated with the topic and use the search engine to seek out all the occurrences of the word. This is much more time-consuming and will also give you many instances of the word which may not be appropriate. Connections may also not be available using this facility, and it may be a case of trying again later, when connections are less busy, or trying to find a direct address to utilise more successfully.

Time and infinite patience are two of the main requirements for 'surfing the net'. It is often a very slow and laborious task, but you do have to remember that it is not just accessing computer systems around the corner, or even in the next county, or country, but WORLD-WIDE!

The Internet offers an e-mail facility and the ability to transmit messages globally. This can be particularly useful for business and organisations, and even on a personal level for those with specific interests and hobbies. Technology is forever developing and advancing. The Internet is part of the business world of today, and will increase its facilities and capabilities with incredible speed. Everyone wants to join in, so it is continuing to grow into the most enormous facility that we can imagine. World-wide communication is no longer a pipe dream: it is a reality through the utilisation of File Transfer Protocol (FTP), and the possibility of promoting, transmitting and receiving data world-wide is here to stay. No longer do we have to contain our business to the area we find ourselves based in. The internet is much more ambitious than that, and is developing both tools and techniques to make it bigger *and* better *and* faster in the foreseeable future.

The Internet does not have any controls imposed on it, nor does it have any restrictions. It provides open access to everyone and everything. Many problems have arisen as a result of this, and within the next year or so controls and restrictions will be implemented to safeguard the users. Access to the Internet is being encouraged in schools, and this is a good thing; but with no safeguards or restrictions, it is too easy to find things which we do not want children to have access to. Pornographic material and other material of an offensive nature can be easily located on the Internet for example.

Browse carefully and be cautious about information that may give you details about purchasing items, or asking you for your credit card details. Take care before you commit yourself to anything, as it may be particularly difficult to stop an item being despatched from the States, once you have pressed the button.

The Internet is a wealth of information, a giant library at your fingertips and often a joy and delight to use. It can also offer unique opportunities to obtain information for projects and homework assignments, the like of which has never been seen before. Make the most of the opportunity to explore and revel in the material at your fingertips, but remember that you can also find yourself in an expensive situation both through the cost of access, as well as through many of the shopping and spending facilities which will be available to you.

Practical Application:

How would you impose restrictions and controls on the Internet? Would it be a 'pay to play' facility or password protection, or even some other method? Do overall tighter controls need to be imposed on all information facilities, or just those of a 'hazardous' nature? How would you impose this?

All our personal information is held on a variety of databases – list the ones you are likely to feature on, and describe how this was achieved. Do you want to be on them? Was it of your own choosing, or not? How would you go about curbing additional entry onto other databases?

> *Produce a detailed report to highlight the area and questions detailed above. Include personal experiences and ideals as you feel appropriate, and also include all relevant material in your portfolio of evidence.*

External databases

External databases exist mainly for references purposes. The Internet provides users with access to many of them, although often they have limited or restricted access as they may be a facility for subscribers only.

Airlines, travel agents and tour operators all need to have access to external databases for availability of flights and holidays. These systems are known as 'real time' systems. That means that if Brenda at Sure Flight books two seats on a flight from Glasgow to Paris, then when Sue at Travel Direct looks to see how many seats are left, there will be two less than there were when Brenda booked them for her customers. The system is constantly being updated to show the current situation.

Other organisations that use external databases include stock exchanges, for dealing in stocks and shares and, on a smaller scale, spare parts for cars. These can be located using the database to ascertain stock levels and availability. Some offer the user the opportunity to interact with the information that the system is showing – like the travel agents, booking the seats on the flight. Others just exist to give you the information that you require, and the additional facilities that may be available are just for the subscribers.

Think of some external databases which you may know about or use. What are they for? How do you use them? Are they interactive, or just for information only? Can anyone access them, or do you have to pay to view? Write a brief description of the facility that you use, and its advantages and disadvantages.

CONCLUSION

COMMUNICATE ELECTRONICALLY USING INFORMATION TECHNOLOGY SOLUTION

Completion of this Unit will demonstrate that you can:

- Utilise electronic communication media for both the transmission and receipt of messages and information;
- Utilise stored information either through a database, or the Internet;
- Communicate effectively with both people and electronic equipment;
- Name a number of different communication facilities;
- Maintain confidentiality at all times;
- Print out messages from the medium used;
- Understand and maximise the potential of any equipment utilised within the organisation as an essential part of today's technology and an integral aspect of the electronic office.

CONGRATULATIONS – YOU HAVE NOW SUCCESSFULLY COMPLETED UNIT EIGHT!

To tie up all the loose ends covered in this Unit, try to complete the Unit 8 exercise to produce additional evidence for inclusion in your portfolio.

EXERCISE

This exercise takes the guise of a minor project, and consists of a comprehensive investigation into the background, capabilities, and possible costs of implementing a suitable system and facilities for the use of e-mail, facsimile, bulletin boards and the Internet, within an organisation.

Research into each element is essential. Similarly, you should provide supporting evidence of the service providers, installation and equipment necessary to facilitate such a system, as well as additional and on-going expenditure to enable continuous use after it has been installed. There are many books and journals available on the market which will help with this aspect. You could also utilise the Internet itself, if you already have access to it, to explore and discover the best facilities and providers available, as well as to find a wealth of information on the subject which will be an asset within the format of this project.

With regard to the facsimile, it does have to be an integral system: one that can be used within the structure of a computer and not a stand-alone facility, so as to become part of a totally electronic communication system.

It would perhaps be a good idea to produce a User's Guide on getting started, and to include all your material and information in here, under suitable sections and/or headings. Tips and explanations could also be included, so that a comprehensive booklet is produced that can be used in conjunction with the implemented system, or when the user needs additional information to help them use the system to its maximum potential.

There is much to investigate and research, and hopefully it will whet your appetite for the taste of things to come in the technological future.

APPENDIX 1

HEALTH AND SAFETY

The main piece of legislation which oversees general health and safety in the workplace is the Health and Safety at Work Act of 1974. This Act looks at both the employers' and the employees' role in helping to maintain a safe place to work.

The employer must ensure that:

- the workplace is safe to work in and without risk to your health;
- the workplace is clean, and that appropriate levels of control apply to dust, noise and fumes;
- any machinery is safe to work with, and that any working practices are followed to maintain the users' safety;
- suitable instructions and/or training for the use of equipment, and supervision where appropriate are provided;
- a health and safety policy is implemented;
- suitable protective uniform as appropriate, or as required within the remit of health and safety rules and regulations, is provided;
- all injuries, diseases and dangerous incidents are reported to the authority concerned;
- first aid facilities and suitable training are provided;
- adequate precautions to prevent fire are taken, as well as to provide ample and suitable means to fight fires;
- provision for suitable and ample means of escape is made;
- a suitable working atmosphere, with a room temperature of at least 16°C is maintained;
- adequate and clean toilet and washroom facilities, appropriate to the number of employees, are provided;
- the lifting of heavy goods or loads is undertaken in a suitable way so as to prevent personal injury;
- the storage of substances and large or dangerous objects is undertaken so as to ensure continuing safety to all.

Employees also need to take some care when at work, and they must also co-operate with the guidelines as follows:

- to follow the organisation's health and safety guidelines;
- to take appropriate action if a hazardous situation arises;
- to ensure that the working area is free from potential hazards

Hazards can be defined as an unsafe situation arising from a failure to use equipment correctly, or in not applying the appropriate working practice. Potential hazards are often less obvious.

Display ergonomics

In order to ensure that users are protected against any potential health risks associated with display equipment, employers now have a number of legal responsibilities to their employees regarding display screen equipment. The Health and Safety (Display Screen Equipment) Regulations 1992 outline these obligations for UK businesses. These regulations can be perceived as a set of guidelines for ensuring that staff can work comfortably and which have to be observed in order to avoid prosecution. Regular checks of display equipment and the provision of suitable training can all be beneficial to the end user, as well as ensuring compliance with the regulations.

These standards facilitate a number of areas within the work situation and one in particular concerns the screen and the image conceived there. There are a number of external factors which are known to affect the quality of the image on the screen. Reflections and glare can be particularly hard to eliminate, as they are often caused by light sources such as windows and office lighting. In addition to making the contents of the display more difficult to read, users unconsciously alter their viewing position in order to minimise the effect of the reflection, which can lead to discomfort and neck strain. Positioning monitors so that there are no direct light sources is not always easy. Often there are floor to ceiling widows on several sides of the room, or in extreme cases no windows at all, and the total light source is coming from a bank of fluorescent lights. There are a number of different types of glare filter of varying effectiveness and cost, which can be used to reduce reflections. Applications which use dark text on a light background have been found to be preferable to light text on a dark background, as this minimises the effect of the glare.

Providing equipment which is optimised for a given work environment goes some way towards reducing the risk of eyestrain, but helping staff to understand how to use their display screen equipment effectively is also an important factor. This can be as simple as providing paper-based information on how to angle a display screen to provide a natural viewing position, and exercises which can be carried out at the user's desk to alleviate eyestrain. It is a good idea to ensure that all users understand how the brightness and contrast controls operate on their equipment. A special workshop, to advise new users on the best way to deal with their own positional and postural requirements from a computer and how to organise their own personal environment or workstation to meet their needs, is often a good way to introduce sensible working practices.

Sometimes it is necessary to ensure that copyholders are provided for users, so that they can place their documents at a convenient distance, and in so doing help their eyes to refocus as little as possible from the document to the screen. It is also suggested that users take a short break from looking at their screen, every hour. This is not a break from work, just a chance to do something different – photocopying, filing, phone calls and other administrative tasks. Also it provides a chance to look long distance so that you can restore some of the control in your eye muscles, as working at a computer is all short and near distance work, and you need to make adequate provision for both short and long distance viewing to keep your eyes in good

Appendix 1

condition. This will help to minimise the effects of working on a computer and help to prevent eyestrain and other resulting eye problems.

Another good exercise is called 'Palming', or holding your hands over your eyes for several seconds. This relaxes the eyes by transferring warmth from your hands to the eye area and also provides users with a break from concentrating on the screen image. Doing neck and shoulder exercises can also help to assist in the reduction of tension in the upper body. This often builds up as a result of working for a long period of time in the same position. Health and Safety regulations now stipulate that employers are also required to pay for eye tests for staff who regularly use display screen equipment, both when they first begin to use displays as part of their job, and at regular intervals thereafter.

The Display Screen Equipment Regulations of 1992 came into force on 1.1.93, and cover all users who regularly work with computer screens. The main points of the Act facilitate the following elements: Display Screen, Keyboard, WorkStation, Chair, Noise, Software, Heat Humidity and Radiation.

The Act stipulated that workstations purchased before 1.1.93 had until 31.12.96 to comply with the requirements and that new workstations from 1.1.93, or those that have been substantially modified, should conform to the requirements immediately.

Display Screen – adjustable, – brightness, contrast, tilt and swivel – no flicker or reflections. Screens should not face a wall or window if at all possible.

Keyboard – separate from the screen with a tiltable facility required. Sufficient room in front of the keyboard for supporting the user's wrists when keying in. The layout of the keys should be clear and free from glare. There are many keyboard variations available on the market to prevent RSI (Repetitive Strain Injury) and to facilitate the user's keyboarding skills.

Workstation – this should be large enough to house the computer equipment provided, as well as to provide sufficient room for the documents that are in use. A document holder is often a useful addition to make working from a document easier. It will also help with eye adjustment from paper to screen and vice versa. A footstool should also be made available to help make the user more comfortable and the desk should be of a height sufficient to allow plenty of legroom.

Chair – this should be adjustable – up and down – with adequate support for the back. Arms are optional but computer users often find it more beneficial not to have arm rests, as this allows them to get closer to the desk and so aid better posture while working.

Noise – this should be kept at a level appropriate so as not to distract normal working or speech. Printers, copiers and faxes should be housed separately to avoid additional background noise, if at all possible. Telephones should also have a volume control option to help reduce the level of noise from ringing phones within the office, especially if there are a vast number situated near each other.

Software – should be installed correctly and be suitable for the job. Licences, security and copyright aspects should be adhered to, as well.

Health and safety

Heat/Humidity and Radiation – it should be a comfortable environment to work in – neither too hot nor too cold. With regard to the electro-magnetic radiation aspect, emissions from display screen equipment have not been proven.

Lighting – should be adjustable so that glare and reflections are eliminated whenever possible. Windows should have blinds so as to prevent additional glare from sunlight.

Electrical safety – all normal electrical/safety precautions should be taken in association with the equipment in use, and wires should be housed out of the way of users, to prevent accidents.

Having considered all of the above elements we should be able to minimise, or even eliminate, many of the problems associated with users of VDU's. The most common problems are eye fatigue and muscular strain caused by incorrect posture and job stress.

Claims for sickness and poor health, such as headaches, neckache, backache and eye disorders are found to be most frequently amongst VDU operators. It is possible to eliminate some of these problems by taking a short break every hour. Undertake some simple preventative measures to ensure that correct posture is achieved, and that the user and the employer both comply with the Act's requirements.

The Act imposes a number of measures that should be complied with, and here are some worth noting:

- assess health and safety risks;
- provide information about the risks and how to reduce them;
- take steps, where possible, to minimise the risk;
- take regular breaks from the computer – by changing activity;
- make eye tests available for regular users of a computer.

Eye discomforts or problems with vision may result from continuous use of a computer when perhaps previously a computer was not being used. Regular checks and the provision of glasses/contact lenses are available, at the employer's expense, should it be found that they have a case to answer to, and that through using a computer, the user's vision has deteriorated.

A term that is often associated with using computers and the provision and building of workstations is **Ergonomics** – the relationship between the workers, the equipment they use, and their working environment.

We can clearly see that often the relationship is poor and needs to be changed. Some employers do not have rigorous checks on the facilities that they offer to their employees, whereas others do everything that they possibly can to make their working life more comfortable. If you have a problem with a piece of equipment that you use regularly, or perhaps insufficient space to work in, inadequate lighting or poor heating facilities, first seek the advice of your line manager or supervisor. If no help is forthcoming, enlist the assistance of your Health and Safety Representative. It is a legal requirement that you, the user, are ensured of the best provision of facilities that are available. If not appropriate action can be taken to remedy this.

Appendix 1

Some concerns associated with working with a computer:

Epilepsy – people concerned should seek professional advice before working with computers.

Facial dermatitis – some users experience facial skin complaints but this is not very common.

Effects on pregnant women – concerns regarding birth defects and miscarriage have been noted, but no link has arisen as a result of tests or research.

RSI – Repetitive Strain Injury – this is the name given to acute pain in the hands, arms, neck and shoulders which can be a result of continuous typing or keyboarding. Posture and hand position, as well as taking regular breaks, all help to alleviate the possibility of pain and strain in our upper limbs.

You can help yourself by sitting correctly and also ensuring that your hands are correctly positioned over the keys. Your wrists should not touch the work surface. If support is required, obtain a wrist rest. When using the mouse, make sure that your wrist and arm are resting on the work surface/mouse mat and that the edge of the surface does not cut across your wrist. Move your papers and documents in order to facilitate a better position which is more comfortable and will help prevent acute pain and possible long-term injury.

Remember

1. Always be sure to switch a machine off before you clean it. Use only the appropriate solutions for the job, and use as directed.

2. Never eat or drink near a computer, in case of accidents.

3. Store bags/briefcases under a desk, never in the gangway or beside you, in case someone falls over them. Never block a doorway, gangway or fire exit, either.

4. Ensure trailing leads are housed correctly – and try to prevent them from crossing a room: follow the skirting board around the room.

5. Get equipment checked regularly, and make sure only competent technicians repair faults.

6. Adhere to the procedure of the organisation/establishment for reporting faults.

Follow all these guidelines and you will maintain an environment that is healthy and safe to work in.

APPENDIX 2

USING PRINT SCREEN AND PAINTBRUSH

In order to provide evidence to substantiate your housekeeping routines, you need to have your word-processing package running - Word 6, Word 97, or similar. Have a NEW document open on the screen, and then MINIMISE it, by using the single down pointing arrow in the top right hand corner of your screen.

Next, you need to open PAINTBRUSH. This can be found under the Accessories group of icons.

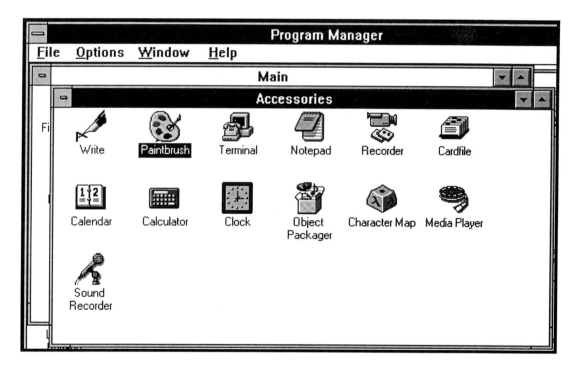

Again, make sure that a new document is open. When this has been done, MINIMISE it so that it is open and available, but not on your screen at the moment.

Finally, you need to go into your A: drive, C: drive or other facility within the File Manager where you save your work, so that you can show exactly what files you have stored there, and how the directories would change should you delete some of the files, or move them to an alternative directory or drive.

The File Manager is usually located within the MAIN group of icons, and is represented by a filing cabinet symbol, as seen below.

File Manager

Double click on the icon and it will open the File Manager facility. Select the appropriate drive from the drives available to you, located at the top of the window.

The next thing to do is to locate the Print Screen button on your keyboard, and to press it just once. Sometimes the screen will flicker, but more often than not nothing visible will happen. What does occur is that a mirror image of what you can see on the screen is sent to the clipboard, a temporary storage facility within the computer, and from here you will be able to pick it up and manipulate it into the form that we are looking for.

Having pressed the Print Screen button, you can now MINIMISE the File Manager facility, ready for use later on.

You next need to double click on the PAINTBRUSH icon,

probably to be found at the bottom of your screen - the usual place when you minimise it. It should pop up in full onto your screen and then by pressing EDIT, from the drop down menu, followed by PASTE, the screen you have just captured on the clipboard should appear on the screen. If it does not appear, repeat the process from pressing the Print Screen button. Practice makes perfect!

Normally, you capture everything that you see on your screen, and you may need to be selective about what you actually want to use, so you need to cut around it. To do this you can use the CUT button: select the pair of scissors with the box attached to them, as this will make cutting it out much simpler.

Press the button, as shown above, and then drag the 'cross' around the area that you want to cut out. Then select EDIT from the menu bar, and click on the word COPY. This means that you leave the current screen in Paintbrush intact, so that if you need to try again, you do not have to recreate it from scratch.

Minimise Paintbrush and then double click on the Word icon, which you should find at the bottom of your screen. A new document should be waiting to receive the image. Press the PASTE button, and the image you cut out should now appear on the screen. Sometimes placing a border around it can tidy it up, as often what you have selected and cut out is just a portion of the whole image or the aspect which is most appropriate. Use the BORDER button to do this, and increase the thickness of the lines around it accordingly. (Border button and facilities are detailed below.)

Appendix 2

You can redo this process as many times as you require, or for different images. Just put a new document on the top each time, ready to capture your print screen image in Paintbrush or similarly in the word-processing document. Soon you will have produced a comprehensive selection of printouts which can prove, without a shadow of a doubt, that you do regular and routine housekeeping exercises; have set up appropriate directories and sub-directories, and that you can also utilise the manifold capabilities of the computer. This exercise will also help familiarise you with the **minimise** and **maximise** facilities and also some of the other software available on the operating system Windows 3.1. **HAVE FUN!**

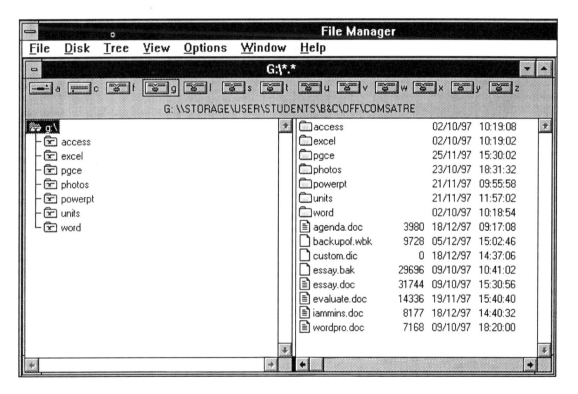

Print screen image showing files and directories in the g: drive

Using Print Screen and Paintbrush

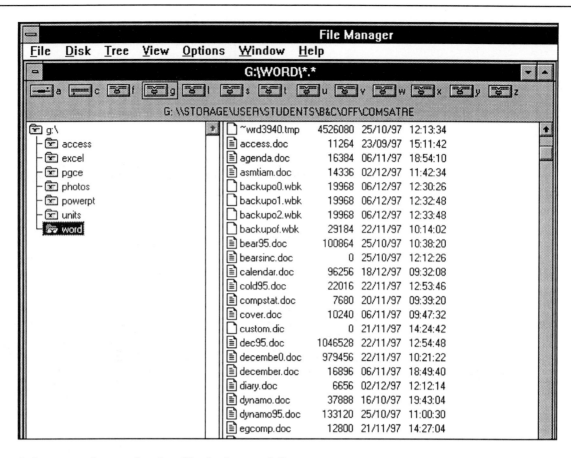

Print screen image showing files in the word directory

APPENDIX 3

USING THE FILE MANAGER IN WINDOWS 3.1

The File Manager is one of the most important facilities within the Windows operating environment. It gives you untold ability to copy, move, rename and delete your files. It also enables you to form your own, or utilise a standard or house style format, for storing files in directories, so that either just you, or other people, can access the files that they may require.

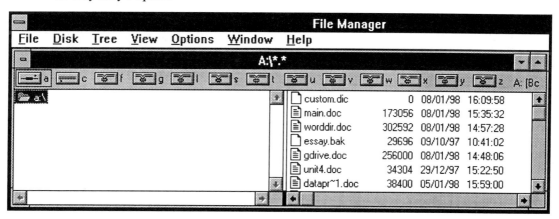

Today, most of us use pre-formatted disks, whereas a few years ago we had to format them 'manually' before we could use them. This formatting facility is to be found within the scope of the File Manager. Select the DISK option from the menu bar, and a series of facilities will appear. Select Format Disk and then follow the directions as prompted on the screen. You can also copy a disk from here, onto another disk, thus giving you a portable back-up facility. Again, you will be prompted on how to go about this procedure by the information which appears on the screen. Make sure that the destination disk you use to receive the copied data doesn't contain anything that you may need, as this will be wiped out when you put the copied data onto it.

You can copy files more easily from a floppy disk to a network facility or to the hard drive, by selecting the appropriate file, and then by using the left mouse key: hold it down and drag it to its required destination. In order for this to be successfully achieved, you need either to have two WINDOWS open on the screen at the same time within the File Manager, or to be able to pop the highlighted file into the correct directory, as shown on the left side of the file manager window and shown below with a box around it. A small document will accompany this process to show that it is actually moving from one place to another, or copying it.

Appendix 3

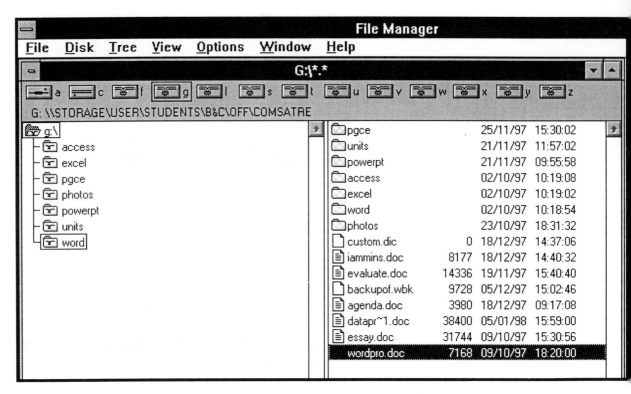

Move tends to mean that it is physically taking it from one directory and placing it into another. This is often the case when they are both within the same drive facility but different directories.

Copy makes a new copy, giving you two copies of the same file, one in the original place and the second in the new destination. The computer makes the decision for you as to whether you need to Move or Copy the file. You are always given a chance to change your mind if you feel that you have made the wrong decision about which facility or file to use. Use this opportunity to confirm and clarify your actions.

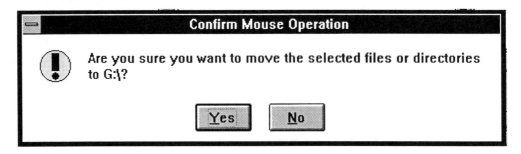

If a copy of the file already exists in the new destination, it will offer you the opportunity to replace it with the new one, but make sure that it is the latest version available and not an old one - check the dates!

Using the File Manager in Windows 3.1

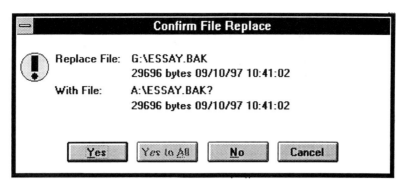

If no previous version can be found, then the computer will happily copy the file to its new destination.

As with most Windows based products, there is more than one way to achieve the required end result. Find the way that you feel happiest using. It may not be the quickest, but may give you a feeling of confidence about what you are doing, and this alone is good, especially as it is easy to make mistakes, and here they can be disastrous!

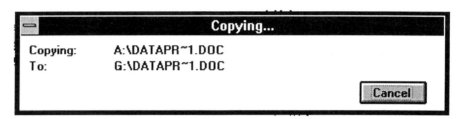

Many of us call a file something in error, or do not conform exactly with the convention or house style required. If you save the file again as the correct name, you then end up with two files. By using the File Manager you can rectify both these situations.

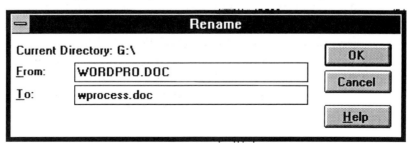

We can rename an existing file by using the RENAME option found under FILE on the Menu Bar. Just type in the required new name, and the computer does the rest!

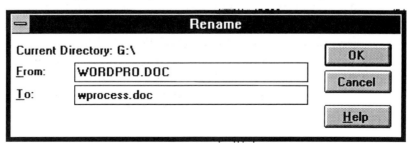

Appendix 3

Remember to type in the correct file extension as well so that the computer will know which application it belongs to when you access it in the future. Also remember that within Windows 3.1, you can only have a maximum of 8 characters in the filename - either letters or numbers, with no punctuation marks or spaces.

Having renamed the file, you may now need to delete any additional ones you created at the time to try to sort out the problem of an incorrect name.

This facility is also found under FILE - Delete.

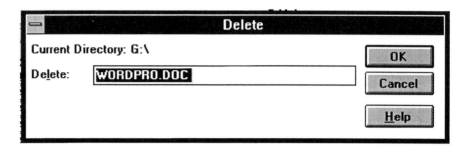

You need to make sure that you have selected the correct file to delete. This will be shown in the dialog box as shown above. Again, you have the opportunity to cancel and re-select a different file if necessary by choosing CANCEL from this first box. If you select OK, a second dialog box appears and again asks if you are *really sure* that this is the correct file to delete. This is a fail-safe mechanism just to make doubly sure that you are deleting the correct one.

The File Manager is a very useful tool, but like most tools, it needs to be handled with extreme care. It is easy to delete the wrong file, to copy or move files to incorrect places, and to re-format or copy over important data on disks. Always check and make sure that you know what you are doing. Seek expert assistance if necessary. As with many of these facilities, there is no recovery process should you make an error.

For ease of use, make sure that you create a simple but effective way of storing your files in directories and sub-directories. (From the FILE menu select Create Directory and call it as required. Make sure that you have hung it from the correct place in your structure to start with. If not, use the Delete facility and start again.) There may be a convention that you have to follow. If not sort out a system for yourself, even if it is nothing more complicated than isolating documents and files by their application – e.g. – Word, Excel, Access and PowerPoint, to list the Microsoft Office Professional suite of programs.

Using the File Manager in Windows 3.1

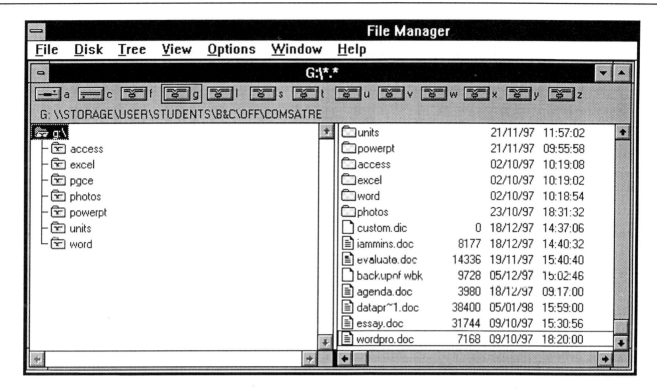

In the diagram above, we can see the ROOT directory – G: and all the sub-directories listed on the left hand side. As we are in the ROOT, they are all listed again on the right with documents currently stored in the G: ROOT, which have not been stored in their correct directories.

Additional information can also be seen on the right, against each filename: size of file, date and time last accessed. The folder shapes (illustrated below – top shape) are directories; the filled documents (below – bottom shape) are documents which the computer recognises with a software package – if you double click on the file name in the File Manager facility, it will open that document for you in its corresponding software package; the clear document (below – middle shape) is a document, but the computer doesn't recognise the file extension, and cannot therefore pigeonhole it to the appropriate software package, so an error message would appear on the screen (see the diagram below) should you double click on it in an attempt to open it from the File Manager.

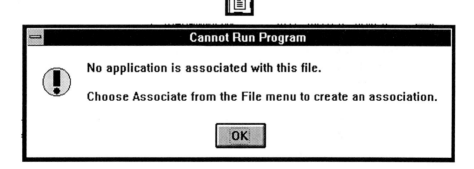

Make the File Manager work for, and with you, as it offers you a vast number of facilities and capabilities which will make your work more effective, and you more efficient!

Appendix 4

COMPETENCE STATEMENTS

The idea behind producing Competence Statements is for the student to produce one to complement every element of the NVQ that they undertake. It should give a complete breakdown of the evidence to be found in the portfolio, which should be listed in order in the top section of the document, and a brief account of how that evidence was produced/achieved in the bottom half. (See examples for an illustration of this.)

It is necessary to give specific details within the competence statement to show the Verifier that you are competent in the area you are working in, and the information you give should be clear. Any cross-references that you use should highlight places where additional material can be found about a certain subject. This cross-referencing facility avoids the duplication of material in your portfolio, and will ensure that all documents appertaining to that subject can easily be traced for additional information or verification.

Paper copies of the Competence Statement are issued in the Candidate Pack, and it is perhaps a good idea to copy a quantity of these so that you can keep rough notes on them for future reference or inclusion in the final version of your Competence Statement. Some colleges/work placements recreate the Competence Statement on the computer, thus giving an electronic format which can be easily updated for each element, or as required.

If you keep notes on the paper copies, it is easy to use them to produce a comprehensive statement when you have finished the whole element. If notes are not kept, you can easily forget important factors or stages which were integral to the production of the end result.

In the bottom section of the Competence Statement, you need to address the following questions:

WHAT

you did to produce the evidence you have detailed above and have included in your portfolio. Include comprehensive information about each aspect or process that you used. You also need to specify

WHEN

you did the work: this is often useful as it will show your progress through the course. Often when you start, all the work is rather confused and brief. As you develop your skills, this will change and become more detailed and comprehensive.

WHERE

you were when you produced it: at college or in your work placement; also where you obtained any information from – books, journals, colleagues, the Internet, etc.

HOW

you went about the processes required to complete the task; if you sought help and from whom, as well as specific details about the initial requirement. It is also vital to mention

WHY

you had to do certain things in order to get the final result.

Make sure that you answer all these questions within the bottom section of the statement, so as to give a comprehensive view of everything that you have done in order to attain a signed element, which will go towards your final award. If you think of any other important information about your work, include that as well. It may just be the details which make the difference between a pass and a fail.

The more detailed and comprehensive the information that you give, the better your Competence Statement will be. Do not repeat yourself just to fill up space on the page. It is better to be brief and concise than longwinded and repetitive. Always check the details that you use, not only in the Competence Statement, but anywhere else that you may quote information. If you specify the use of a key sequence, run through it using the words you have written and double check that it really does work and produce the end result that you are trying to obtain. There is nothing worse than following instructions that do not work. Running through any procedures to check them will also help you to remember how they work and what they do, and hopefully will assist you in the future when you need to recall this procedure. If you quote from books and journals, make sure that you specify your source, and use quotation marks where relevant.

Competence Statements are never a popular aspect of the NVQ syllabus, but with a little preparation and some notes to work from, they should soon become a doddle for everyone, and will definitely help to assist with the verification process and your overall attainment of the qualification that you are seeking – NVQ Level II in Using IT.

CLAIM TO COMPETENCE

NVQ IN USING I.T. LEVEL 2

UNIT 5

Element 5.1

List the type of evidence obtained and where it is located:
(THIS IS AN EXAMPLE ONLY)

(1) Health and Safety leaflet
(2) VDU Health and Safety article
(3) Working with Computers homework
(4) Group assignment for Health and Safety
(5) Presentation material for Health and Safety group work
(6) Additional material for Health and Safety

N.V.Q.

LEVEL II IN USING I.T.

- The numbered items above should correspond with the evidence that you have in your portfolio.
- Make sure that the number and description match and that they are in the correct order so that the Verifier can easily find any piece of work that you have produced and have detailed in the list above.
- It may be that you have many more pieces of work or evidence to include. Number them all carefully and file in the appropriate section of your portfolio.

Details of work carried out:

In this section of the Competence Statement you need to address WHAT you did to produce the evidence you have detailed above. Include comprehensive information about each aspect or process that you used. You also need to specify **WHEN** you did the work. This is often useful as it will show your progress through the course. Often when you start, all the work is rather confused and brief, but as you develop your skills this will change and become more detailed and comprehensive. **WHERE** you were when you produced it – at college or in your work placement and also where you obtained any information from - journals, colleagues, the Internet, etc. **HOW** you went about the processes required to complete the task. If you sought help and from whom, as well as specific details about the initial requirement. It may also be vital to mention **WHY** you had to do certain things in order to get the final result.

Make sure that you answer all these questions within this section of the statement so as to give a comprehensive view of everything that you have done in order to attain a signed element, which will go towards your final award. If you think of any other important information about the work you are talking about, include that as well: it may just be the details which make the difference between a pass and a fail.

Candidate's signature .... **Date** ....

Assessor's signature .... **Date** ....

Competence Statements

CLAIM TO COMPETENCE

NVQ IN USING IT   LEVEL 2

UNIT 1

Element 1.1

List the type of evidence obtained and where it is located:
(THIS IS AN EXAMPLE ONLY)

1) Copy of the table I had to produce for my supervisor while at my work placement.

Details of work carried out:

While at my work placement, using the software Word 6 for Windows (a word-processing package produced by Microsoft and part of the Office Professional suite of programmes) I was asked to produce a table which would contain details of all the personnel in a given department, together with their addresses and phone numbers for use in an emergency.

I started by opening a NEW file, and using the Menu Bar I clicked on the word TABLE and selected Insert Table from the drop-down menu. I had previously worked out how many columns and rows I would need to accommodate everyone, and using the increase arrow for both the columns and rows in the dialogue box, increased them accordingly. I next selected the AutoFormat button to help decide on the LOOK of the table. I chose the LOOK – GRID 1 – which gave me a border around each cell as well as around the whole of the outside edge of the table.

Once the table was in place, I was able to fill it up with the information I had been given, treating each cell as if it was part of an ordinary document - editing and amending as required. Once I had completed this keying in, I printed out the required number of copies, again by using the Menu Bar – File – Print and increasing the number of copies to accommodate the number I required. I also made sure that the button was shown against ALL, so that I would get the whole document printed out. Once the printing was finished, I then distributed them as directed by my supervisor via the internal mail system, having first written each recipient's name on the front.

Candidate's signature ....   Date ....

Assessor's signature ....   Date ....

Appendix 5

PERSONAL AND WITNESSED STATEMENTS

Personal Statements are statements which the student produces to detail exactly what work they have undertaken and how they achieved the end results specified and which, perhaps, can be found in the portfolio of evidence.

Personal Statements are usually a record of the work which was given as tasks during a period of work experience. Hardcopy evidence may accompany various aspects, but this is not always possible due to security and confidentiality. Always check first before you take a copy of anything, it may be TOP SECRET!

Witnessed Statements are similar to personal ones but are compiled by your supervisor. They are, however, sometimes drafted by you, as you may be more aware of what you have been doing within the realms of your work experience than they are. The statement needs to have a list of all the aspects that you have tackled. These can be numerous and varied. At the bottom of the statement, leave room for a signature and date, and when you have double-checked the contents, ask your supervisor to sign it for you as a true and accurate testimony of the work that you have done. You may also sign it to verify this statement. Always put a date on your statement so that it can be treated as current. Old work is not always valid.

Sometimes you can utilise working experiences from a previous job within the realms of this course, and it may be possible to get your previous employer/supervisor to produce a statement which will detail all the work you carried out while you were with them. This can count towards your NVQ qualification, but again it does need to be fairly recent for it to be valid. Where technology is concerned trends, skills and competencies can easily go out-of-date, and be superseded by newer and more powerful facilities and abilities.

Before you assume that you can include any personal or witnessed statements check with you tutor to confirm that what you are seeking to include is appropriate to the contents of the course, and not a waste of time.

These statements can be a useful way of attaining extra recognition for work that you have undertaken previously, and which is relevant, either as part of your full-time job or as part of your work experience. Work experience is classified as an essential part of the syllabus of this course. Never be afraid to ask if an aspect or element of it can be counted as part of your award: the more experience and work associated with the elements of the course, the better. It is a VOCATIONAL award, after all!

Appendix 6

UNITED KINGDOM LEGISLATION

DATA PROTECTION ACT 1984

What Is The Data Protection Act?

The Data Protection Act of 1984 is a piece of legislation that is currently applicable to us all in the United Kingdom, in some form or other. It relates only to personal data held electronically about living people and is based on eight main principles:

(1) Data must be obtained lawfully and fairly;

(2) Data must be held only for specific purposes – these have to be defined at registration;

(3) Data must not be used for any purpose other than those specified;

(4) Data must be adequate, relevant and not excessive – the minimum to meet the specified purpose;

(5) Data must be accurate and kept up-to-date;

(6) Data must be held only as long as necessary;

(7) Data should be accessible by those to whom it belongs, and is about, and should be amended, corrected or deleted as appropriate;

(8) Security systems must be in place to ensure that no unauthorised access by users is possible, who may alter, destroy or disclose confidential information.

The Data Protection Act was introduced in 1984, and is administered by the Data Protection Registrar. He is an independent officer who reports directly to Parliament and ensures that the information used is correct. The Data Protection Act is concerned with 'personal data' which is processed electronically. The Act gives individuals certain rights, as well as making sure that the people who use and record the personal data on the computer are honest about that use, and follow the rules and regulations in association with the Act.

Definitions

Personal Data

This means the information relevant to and about living people. It can be as little as a name and address, or it can be vast amounts of confidential and personal data.

Appendix 6

Automatically Processed

Data and information which can be processed electronically using a computer.

Data Users

These are people who control and use the data on a computer. Examples of these may include:

(i) a large or small company in the public or private sector;

(ii) a sole trader or partnership;

(iii) an individual.

Data Subjects

These are the people that the data relates to.

Registration

If you wish to use this information, you must first be registered by the Data Protection Registrar. You are charged a standard fee and this covers your use of the information for 3 years. You can obtain a DPR4 which is a shortened version of the registration form from the registrar's office. It is a crime not to register and you can be fined up to £5,000 plus costs, and can even be tried in a Magistrate's Court, should you not comply with the requirements of the Act, or register promptly.

There are a few people and facilities who do not have to register and these are as follows:

(a) computers used and data held in connection only with personal, family or household affairs or recreational use;

(b) data used only for preparing text in documents;

(c) data used for wages and pensions, accountancy or keeping records of purchases;

(d) data used for distributing articles or information to data subjects;

(e) data held by a sport or recreational club that is not a Limited company.

It is always better to register, if in doubt. When you apply to register, you have to give certain information about yourself and the data you are going to store, as you are going to be the user.

This may take the form of:

(a) why you wish to use it;

(b) where you are going to get the information from;

(c) who the information is going to be shown or given to;

(d) whether you are going to transfer any of the data you retrieve or store to other countries.

If the Registrar ever feels that any of these rules and regulations are being neglected or abused, he has the right to take action against you and severe penalties and fines may be enforced as a result of non-compliance.

For More Information On What Is Stored About You As An Individual:

If, as an individual, you feel that you would like to find out what information the Data Protection register holds about you, it is open to public inspection, or you have the right to make a written request asking for information. A small fee of £10.00 is normally charged, and you should receive a response within 40 days. If for some reason you are denied access to this information, you are entitled to make an appeal to the Registrar, or you can ask for a court order so that you can gain access. The same applies if you feel what is in the data is false or untrue.

EUROPEAN UNION LEGISLATION

EUROPEAN UNION DIRECTIVE ON PROTECTION OF PERSONAL DATA 1995

The aim of this piece of legislation is to make it possible for the free movement of personal data within the European Union (EU), and to minimise the differences between national protection laws throughout the European Union.

The benefits of such legislation will ensure that the subjects of any data being processed within the EU will have equal protection of their rights. This is with special regard to privacy, regardless of which member state is carrying out the processing.

It is also hoped that this legislation will prevent EU rules being avoided or disregarded when data is being transferred to a non-EU country.

Appendix 7

ON PROGRAMME TUTORIAL SHEETS

These sheets have been designed to be used in conjunction with any forms that your education establishment currently uses to document a student's progress throughout a course. It is a dual use form, which offers both the tutor and the student an opportunity to complete various boxes, either before or during the tutorial, so that an accurate record of achievement is obtained from each tutorial session attended.

Basic information is written at the top – course code, name and date. The three academic terms are already written out for you, so that you can just cross out the ones which are not appropriate at the time of completion.

The first box contains details about the student's overall progress since either the last tutorial or the initial interview before acceptance on the course.

The information on the form can be completed in full, or in note form, whichever you feel to be more acceptable or appropriate.

Marks for work submitted, or grades for exams, are entered in the second box. The description of the work, or the exam sat, is put into the left-hand side and the mark/grade achieved is added next to it. If no mark/grade has yet been given, write the date it is expected by in the right-hand side box.

Tasks or unit exercises can be detailed in box three, and dates when they are expected to be achieved by can accompany these. It is often good to give out dates so that the student has something to aim for, and can plan his or her workload accordingly. It is, however, vital to remember that whatever is discussed during a tutorial must be **agreed** by both parties for it to work successfully, and this includes dates and deadlines!

The overall progress and assessment of the student goes into box four, and reflects what has been achieved with regard to the unit exercises, or other appropriate work appertaining to the course syllabus.

Work experience is box five, and this will detail venue, dates and a contact name. Comments from either the student, or the contact, can be included here, so that a comprehensive overview of the work experience situation can be assessed, during the course of the tutorial.

The reverse of the sheet is for the student to complete with general comments, problems or questions that they wish to raise during the course of the tutorial, or for the tutor to write comments about the current situation with regard to the student's progress.

Both the tutor and student need to sign the sheet and date it. This completed sheet can then be included in the portfolio of evidence to document progress during the course.

Tutorials are normally held once each academic term, or semester, according to the way your college works. It is important to remember that should you need to seek additional expert assistance or help, about either a course-related or personal problem, that you seek it immediately and do not wait until your next planned tutorial. By then it could be too late to remedy the situation.

The usual time allocated to a tutorial is normally between 20-30 minutes, but more or less can be given, as the situation dictates. The venue needs to be convivial, and be free from interruptions. The time needs to be mutually agreed, with room for flexibility and negotiation, again as the need arises – often things crop up at the last minute, and the time/date cannot be kept.

Tutorials, like appraisals within the working world, offer a two-way form of communication and also the opportunity to discuss frankly your fears and expectations and for your tutor or supervisor to praise and offer support over the forthcoming period. It will help you to recognise your strengths and weaknesses and put into place suitable objectives and goals to be met, and to agree a plan of action which will facilitate your course work and also the requirements of any job or work experience related to it.

Make the most of this opportunity to discuss things on a one-to-one basis. Prepare in advance the things that you want to discuss in detail, and make notes about the rest to remind you later on. If you follow this advice, you will certainly get the most out of this tutorial opportunity and this in turn will help you to achieve your ultimate aim – NVQ Level II in Using IT.

Appendix 7

ON PROGRAMME TUTORIAL INFORMATION

COURSE CODE:
STUDENT NAME:
DATE OF TUTORIAL:
ACADEMIC PERIOD: AUTUMN / SPRING / SUMMER

PROGRESS AND ACHIEVEMENTS SINCE LAST TUTORIAL/INTERVIEW:

MARKS FOR WORK SUBMITTED/EXAM GRADES:

Work submitted and date	Marks/grades

AGREED TASKS/UNIT EXERCISES AND ASSOCIATED TARGET DATES:

Tasks to do	Target date

UNIT EXERCISES ATTEMPTED:

Progress:
Overall assessment:

WORK EXPERIENCE:

Venue:	Dates:	Contact:
Comments:		

On programme tutorial sheets

GENERAL COMMENTS:

Tutor's signature: _____ **Date:** _____

Student's signature: _____ **Date:** _____

GLOSSARY

OF NVQ AND IT TERMS AND ABBREVIATIONS

Assessor	Tutor or lecturer with relevant qualifications (D32 and D33), who can observe you working and grade your written work appropriately for the award you are working towards.
CD ROM	Compact Disk - Read Only Memory - a disk in read only format used as a backing store to hold large amounts of data, or used for software applications to be stored on and then installed into your computer system.
Copyright	It is illegal to copy software. You must have an appropriate licence for its use. Anything contrary to this is in breach of copyright law.
Data Protection Act	This act was made law in 1984, to protect and control the storage of personal data on computer systems.
e-mail	Electronic Mail - transmission and receipt of messages from one user to another, via a computer network. It can be on a local scale, or a global one.
Evidence	Hardcopy or paperwork which you, the student, have collected, created and collated to construct a portfolio to substantiate your knowledge and learning.
External Verification	The sampling of students' work by a representative of the awarding body to ensure that what has been produced is authentic and appropriate for the award in question.
Fax	Facsimile - electronic means of sending messages from one place to another by a scanning process and using telephone lines as the means of data transfer.
Hardcopy	Paper version of an electronically created file.
Hardware	The 'bits you can kick' - the machinery parts of the computer which will include the keyboard, the central processing unit and the printer.

Glossary of NVQ and IT terms and abbreviations

Health and Safety	Aspects which you have to consider when working, which will ensure your personal well-being as well as that of those around you.
Housekeeping	Routine backup procedures as well as the deleting or moving of old files no longer required. Maintenance and upkeep of the status of the computer system at all times. Data security and integrity must also be kept intact.
Internal Verification	Sampling of work produced by students, by an independent college assessor.
Internet	A super-network – the linking of many computer networks world wide to exchange information and to offer the facility of interaction between users. Access to the network is via Service Providers.
Intranet	The linking of computers within an organisation - a form of networking facility, again for the exchange of information and ideas, but within the confines of an organisation.
IT	Information Technology – the utilisation and coming together of electronic functions to enable the processing of data. It may also encompass aspects of telecommunications, computing and digital technology.
ITITO	Information Technology Industry Training Organisation – organisation that produced the Standards utilised in this book for the NVQ syllabus.
LCCI	London Chamber of Commerce and Industry - awarding body for the NVQ Level II in Using IT qualification.
Licence	The authority given to users by the software company to use their product legally. They can be specific for either single or multi users, computer, network or site. If you do not have a licence for a piece of software it is not legal, and you should not attempt to use it.
Modem	Modulator – DEModulator - this is a device for communication, and the sending and receiving of messages electronically, through the use of telephone lines. Digital signals are converted and passed over the telephone lines to the other end, where they are received and converted back again.
NVQ	National Vocational Qualification – a vocational and work-based course which is assessed on coursework as opposed to sitting examinations for the attainment of the award. A flexible approach to learning.

Glossary

Peripheral	Devices which are attached to a computer for specialist tasks – a joystick and a mouse are examples of these.
Portfolio	The file that you create which contains the evidence you have produced for attaining the NVQ award.
RAM	Random Access Memory – this is the part of the computer which holds software, programs and data that you input, on a temporary basis. It is volatile – as soon as you switch off the machine, any aspects not saved correctly will be lost.
ROM	Read Only Memory – a basic part of the operating system of the computer, and essential for its starting up procedures. You can only read from this part of the memory, you cannot edit it, add to or delete it.
RSA	Royal Society of Arts - awarding body for the NVQ Level II in Using IT qualification.
Sabotage	The wanton destruction of programs, data and files on a computer system, financial gain.
Virus	A rogue computer program which can cause destruction, damage and corruption to data, files and information stored on a computer system. It can replicate itself to cause more damage in other machines, or can lie dormant for years waiting for a trigger to set it running again. It can easily be passed from one machine to another if it goes undetected and unchecked.
WWW	World Wide Web: also known as the Internet and the Information Superhighway.

NVQ TRANSLATION BY ELEMENT

CORE ELEMENTS

Unit 1		
1.1	Prepare Use of Information Technology	General competency in the use of computer equipment.
1.2	Monitor Use of Information Technology	Continuous use of computer equipment safely and within the confines and facilities of the organisation.
1.3	Conclude Use of Information Technology	Use of Windows operating system, software, directories and floppy and hard drive facilities.
Unit 2		
2.1	Enter Data to Create and Update Files	Creation of new files; use of existing files; opening and closing of files and windows; file naming conventions.
2.2	Produce Required Document by Manipulating Data	Production of files and documents using appropriate software and its facilities.
2.3	Output Specified Document to Destination	Printing of documents and competent use of printing facilities.
Unit 3		
3.1	Maintain the Equipment	Cleaning and general maintenance of computer equipment; knowledge of fault reporting procedures; Health and Safety legislation and requirements.
3.2	Maintain Data File Structures	Creation of directories; sub-directories; back-up facilities and general housekeeping procedures.
3.3	Maintain Media and Documentation Libraries	Observation of copyright legislation; knowledge of appropriate licensing facilities, requirements and restrictions. Storage methods, media and facilities.

NVQ translation by element

Unit 4	
4.1 Contribute to Improving the Use of Information Technology	Continuous improvement and competence in the use of appropriate software.
4.2 Improve Own Use of Information Technology	Identification of weaknesses and ways of possible improvement. Use of manuals and on-line help facilities to compliment this.
4.3 Contribute to Effective Use of Information Technology	Appropriate use of IT facilities to aid daily working practices.
4.4 Establish and Maintain Working Relationships with Other Colleagues	Communication at all levels - formal and informal, oral and written, plus establishing effective working relationships.
Unit 5	
5.1 Monitor and Maintain Health and Safety Within the Working Environment	Awareness of Health and Safety aspects and implementation where appropriate.
5.2 Monitor and Maintain the Security of the Working Environment	Awareness of security measures - passwords, specific access limitations, rights and privileges.
5.3 Monitor and Maintain Data Security in the Working Environment	Data Protection Act; EU data protection law; organisation's legislation and/or restrictions.

OPTIONAL ELEMENTS

Unit 6

6.1	Enter Numerical Data to Create and Update Files	Competent use of spreadsheets.
6.2	Produce Required Model by Manipulating Data	Production of a spreadsheet for a required purpose.
6.3	Produce Graphical Representation from Numerical Information	Production of graphical representation of the spreadsheet.
6.4	Output Specified Model to Destination	Hardcopy printouts of the spreadsheet and graphical representation files.

Unit 7

7.1	Enter Data to Create and Update Images	Competent use of a graphics package.
7.2	Produce Required Graphical Image by Manipulating Data	Production of a file using a graphics package.
7.3	Output Specified Image to Destination	Hardcopy printouts of the graphics package documents.

Unit 8

8.1	Transmit Messages Using Information Technology	Competent use of e-mail, fax and Internet facilities to send messages/information, plus appropriate hardcopy evidence.
8.2	Receive Messages Using Information Technology	Competent use of e-mail, fax and Internet facilities to receive messages/information, plus appropriate hardcopy evidence.
8.3	Access Stored Information System	Competent use of facilities to access stored information, plus appropriate hardcopy evidence.

SUPPLEMENTARY UNIT SCENARIOS

UNIT 1

You have been offered a two week temporary post at a local organisation that specialises in Market Research, as a secretary to one of the main management teams, as the usual secretary is off sick.

You turn up on the Monday morning at 9 a.m. and are bombarded with a variety of tasks to do by lunchtime – how do you prioritise them *and* cope with the unknown computer system which confronts you?

The tasks you are given are:

1. Write a letter to Mr Simpson accepting his invitation to lunch next Wednesday (MD).
2. Photocopy a batch of questionnaires for local distribution by canvassers at the shopping precinct for the next day (Market Research Department).
3. Send a memo to organise a routine maintenance service for the photocopier which has been jamming more often recently (Contact Resources Department).
4. Produce a staff rota of canvassers for the next two weeks, showing days and times as well as venues for work – for distribution at the next staff meeting – TBA (Market Research Department).
5. Prepare an agenda for the next staff meeting.
6. Organise the time and venue for the next staff meeting and send out a memo to everyone connected, advising them of the meeting.

Remember, each task you have been given needs to be addressed as soon as possible, but first you have to access the computer system in order to be able to carry out any of this work. Detail how you would go about this and then how to produce each of the documents, or tasks detailed above.

Actually produce the documents specified and give suggestions as to how to avoid this situation of "the unknown computer system" happening again in the future to another unsuspecting temp.

UNIT 2

You have been called in to assist the sales department with its end of year figures and to help with the production of a report which incorporates relevant spreadsheet details, as well as a graph, into the text of the main document.

There is a standard template used for this report. Ascertain where it can be found (make this up) and how you would go about amending the data so that it is appropriate for your current task.

Give details of how to achieve the integration of the spreadsheet into the report, and also how to edit the figures once in the body of the text.

Produce an example of such a document.

UNIT 3

Prepare a number of OHP slides on "How to Look After Your Computer" for a presentation to a small group of new VDU/WP operators who have just joined your organisation.

Break the topic down into a number of different tasks/stages and explain on each slide what you need to do and why. Also give clear instructions on how to do it – safely. Include graphics where possible.

Produce a set of these slides and give the presentation to other members of your class/dept., and get their feedback on your presentation. (PowerPoint or a similar presentation package is good to use for this exercise.)

UNIT 4

Within your college or workplace, design and create a database to log and maintain all the software packages, purchases, versions and upgrades, types of licence held and where each package can be accessed – by machine reference. Input dates of purchase and upgrades plus contact names as you feel appropriate.

Produce suitable documentary evidence for supporting the creation of the database and also a guide as to its capabilities.

This may be especially helpful when producing reports to detail the availability of software and how to generate the most appropriate report to meet your needs.

Update and maintain the database over a period of time. Highlight any advantages and disadvantages, plus any amendments you would make.

During the design phase, work alongside your colleagues to ascertain their requirements with regards to the database, and include them in any program testing. It is a fundamental requirement that the facility is easy to use. Offer support and training as appropriate, as well as documentary evidence as a reference for them in the future.

Supplementary unit scenarios

UNIT 5

You suspect one of the junior members of your computer technicians' team of making pirate copies of one of your new games packages and selling it to staff in the canteen, for personal profit, during the lunch-break.

Detail how you would tackle this situation. Think before you act (you could have got your facts wrong) and what you would do to prevent this from happening in the future.

Cover all relevant issues from improved security measures right through to necessary disciplinary procedures of personnel, and even future vetting of new recruits.

Write a comprehensive report to your Head of Department outlining the problem, your solution and the way forward. Do not get too bogged down with the personnel issues – pursue rather the security aspects: now, and in the future.

UNIT 6

Your organisation is to hold an exhibition of its products for existing and potential customers during May, and you have been asked to organise some additional help for specific areas which already have a heavy workload. These areas are catering, maintenance and general administration.

The event is to be held in a series of marquees on the recreation area at the back of the main site, and extra help for the maintenance department will be an asset in rigging stands and moving equipment once the marquees have been professionally erected.

The catering department is always busy and it is planned to hold both buffet lunches and sit down meals so that staff can entertain visitors, or just have a snack, if by themselves. Coffee and tea will be available throughout the day. Extra help preparing the food, and also serving it, will be essential.

General administration covers a multitude of sins – from paperwork and invitations, to greeting visitors, showing them where to go and just about everything in between.

Your task is to liaise with each department and ascertain their expected requirement – the number of extra "pairs of hands" – and you have to compile a spreadsheet so that you work within your budget for extra help for the event, of £2500.

You have been able to ascertain that contracted staff earn the following rates:
Maintenance workers earn £4.10 per hour;
Catering staff earn £4.60 per hour;
General administrators earn £4.15 per hour.

The extra help is expected to be required 2 days prior to the event, and for 6 hours per day; 10 hours on the day itself, and 4 hours the day after to help clear up – thus making a total of 26 hours per person. There may be some extra help required by general administration and less by catering, as most of their work is in preparation, rather than after the event.

Check your calculations to ensure that everyone earns within the minimum wage bracket set by your organisation of £4.15 per hour. If this is not so, adjust your figures to reflect a suitable increase in pay per hour to meet this criteria. Remember that you cannot go over-budget!

Show your calculations by department and also the number of extra "pairs of hands" they can expect for the event. Also, show the total cost of the hired help for the whole event. Display your calculations and formulae as well. Print out both the spreadsheet showing the figures and one to show the formula. Make sure that it will all fit onto one page – increase and decrease column widths as appropriate.

UNIT 7

Using a graphics package that you are familiar with, produce a company logo to illustrate the new corporate identity and colours – red, blue and grey of your company. The company wants to be able to use this logo on all its headed paper, brochures and anywhere where it will be instantly recognised, so it should be resizable as necessary. Choose whatever you feel will be applicable to illustrate and represent your company image, but stick to the colours mentioned above.

Give instructions on how to use and input the logo when saved to floppy disk, hard drive or network facility, so that it is readily available for all members of staff to utilise until the new stationery comes back from the printers.

UNIT 8

Take a topic of interest to you and design a Web Site/Home Page. It is to include a number of useful details as well as basic information about the subject. Show where hyperlinks to other pages/information would be and detail the information accessed there. Include any suitable graphics and narrative to help the user access and browse your topic.

Produce the detail using a package you are familiar with. This is an exercise only. You are not expected to produce an actual Web Site/Home Page, just to illustrate how you would go about the design/creation of it.

BIBLIOGRAPHY AND REFERENCES

Business Basics - Organisational Behaviour - Various - BPP - 1995

Organisational Behaviour - Andrzej Huckynski & David Buchanan - Prentice Hall 1991

Management Teams - Why They Succeed or Fail - R. M. Belbin - Butterworth-Heinemann 1981

ACKNOWLEDGEMENTS

ITITO – for the use of their *Standards for the NVQ Level II in Using IT* – Issue 4.0 April 1996.

Clip Art graphics from Microsoft Office Professional.

File Manager images and icons recreated through the utilisation of the Paint accessory in Windows.